Spitfire
in action

by Jerry Scutts

**illustrated by Don Greer &
Rob Stern**

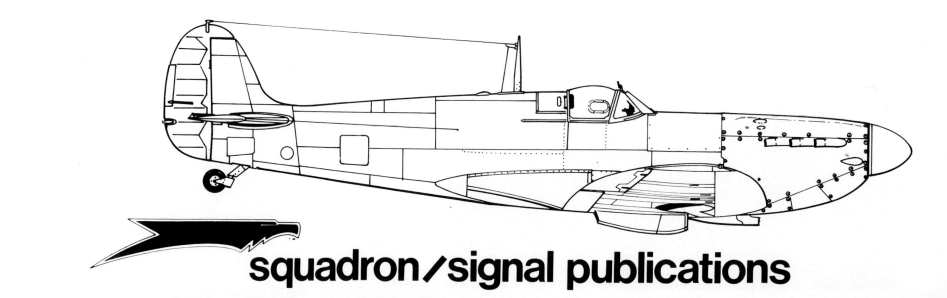

squadron/signal publications

Two Spitfire Mk. IXc fighters of No. 312 (Czech) Sqdn. climb out of cloud over the famed Dover cliffs on their way to provide air cover to the troops invading Normandy, 6 June 1944. The distinctive top and bottom D-Day black and white bands were ordered for all Allied aircraft flying over the Normandy area.

ISBN 0-89747-092-3

If you have any photographs of the aircraft, armor, soldiers or ships of any nation, particularly wartime snapshots, why not share them with us and help make Squadron/Signal's books all the more interesting and complete in the future. Any photograph sent to us will be copied and the original returned. The donor will be fully credited for any photos used. Please send them to: Squadron/Signal Publications, Inc., 1115 Crowley Dr., Carrollton, TX 75011-5010.

Photo credits:

The author would like to thank the following individuals and organizations for assisting with photographs to illustrate this volume:

Paul Allonby	Aeroplane Monthly
Dana Bell	ECP Armees (ECPA)
L. Beckford	Flight International
Harry Holmes	Ministry of Defence
L. L. Peeters	RAF Museum
Bruce Robertson	Imperial War Museum
Chris Shores	United States Air Force
Frank Smith	Vickers
Roger Warren	Gen. Sikorsky Historical Institute
	Polish Air Force

In the summer of 1938, No. 19 Squadron at Duxford became the first Spitfire unit. On 4 May the following year, the Cambridgeshire airfield was opened to the press to record the new fighter for posterity. Points of interest visible here include both flat and bulged cockpit canopies, and flash suppressors fitted to the machine guns on the nearest aircraft, which lacks an individual code letter. Next in line is WZ-C, K9912. (Flight International)

Spitfire Mk I

At the time of its inception there was nothing to match the Supermarine Spitfire for sheer grace of line and, while one might argue its claim to be the most esthetically appealing single seat fighter to emerge from the Second World War, there are surely few contenders for the title. With a combat record second to none, the Spitfire exemplified the part played by the RAF to gain final victory in that conflict, and to the British nation was far more than just another airplane that had helped to win the war. People saw it as the single weapon that had preserved a way of life at a time when everything they held dear was in the greatest danger of being forcibly changed forever. It mattered little to the man in the street that the Spitfire's part in the Battle of Britain was numerically less than that of the Hurricane, for it was the Supermarine fighter that caught the public imagination in a way that was probably unique.

Certainly few fighter aircraft were more aptly named; in squadron service when war broke out, Spitfires were still coming off the production lines when hostilities ceased, a record matched by only a handful of types on either side. But perhaps no greater proof of the Spitfire's longevity is needed than to record that even today preserved examples are still meeting stringent RAF airframe X-ray tests necessary for them to fly as part of the Battle of Britain Memorial Flight.

Brainchild of the brilliant designer Reginald J. Mitchell, whose high-performance racing seaplanes laid the foundations for a new generation of military interceptor fighters, the Spitfire stemmed from Air Ministry Specification F.7/30 issued in 1931, for a new fighter to replace the Bristol Bulldog. Supermarine's contender, the heavy, gull-winged Type 224, was one of eight designs submitted to meet the very broad outline of the official requirement. The machine bore little resemblance to either the 'S' series Schneider Trophy racers or the later Type 300 Spitfire prototype, being only a design progression. As it failed to win the design competition and showed little development potential in its original form, Mitchell undertook a further study to be known as the Type 300 - which fortuitously coincided with development of the 1,000 hp Rolls-Royce PV-12 engine, later known as the Merlin. Subsequent specifications issued in 1935 (F.37/34 calling for a four-gun armament and F.10/35, for 6 to 8 guns) found the Type 300, powered by the new R-R engine, a strong contender. For Supermarine, Air Ministry approval of the Type 300 and resultant military contracts meant the difference between public financing and company funding.

By working closely with the engine manufacturers, the Air Ministry and RAE Farnborough, Supermarine eliminated a number of shortcomings in the basic design and began work on a prototype in March 1935, following construction of a wooden mock-up. Twelve months later the prototype, K5054, was transported to Eastleigh airport in Hampshire for its maiden flight with Vickers' chief test pilot 'Mutt' Summers at the controls. On the morning of 5 March the prototype Spitfire was found to fly as well as its graceful lines had indicated.

On 3 July 1936 the initial contract for 310 Spitfires - later increased to 510 - was signed. Mitchell's untimely death on 11 June meant that he never saw the first production Spitfires, but he died confident that the Spitfire was equal to, if not better than, any other fighter in the world. Detail development and production of the Spitfire was covered by Spec F.16/36 and the program proceeded under the guidance of Mitchell's able colleague, Joseph Smith. To Supermarine fell the huge task of organizing the construction of hundreds of complex aircraft at a time when production on such a scale was something quite new to the aircraft industry.

A low wing monoplane of conventional construction, the Spitfire employed an all-metal stressed skin fuselage and single-spar wing with fabric-covered control surfaces. Exceptionally clean cowling lines were achieved by locating the radiator under the starboard wing, with a smaller circular section oil cooler under the port wing to give the characteristic asymmetrical appearance.

Before and after it had been joined by production Spitfires, K5054 undertook an extensive test program which eventually totalled 151.30 flying hours. It was written off in a crash at Farnborough on 4 September 1939, by which time nearly a dozen RAF squadrons had Spitfires. The first operational unit was No. 19 Squadron, based at Duxford in Cambridgeshire, which accepted its first aircraft in August 1938. Conversion to a high-performance monoplane from biplane Gloster Gauntlets brought No.19's pilots a number of problems, not least of which was remembering to lower the landing gear. As the premier Spitfire unit, No. 19 became the service evaluation squadron for the type and to everyone's credit, there were no fatalities during this demanding but all-important pre-war period.

Throughout the rest of 1938 and into 1939, production and service deliveries proceeded. By 3 September 1939 the RAF had taken 306 Spitfires on charge and 36 had been written off; 187 were distributed among operational squadrons, which were at that time: Nos. 19, 41, 54, 65, 66, 72, 602 and 611, plus 603 and 609 (partially equipped).

RAF squadron reports and manufacturer's development flying led to a number of production line changes to Spitfire Mk Is before the war: the flat cockpit canopy of the early machines was replaced by the familiar curved molding; armor plate protection was added to the rear engine bulkhead; an engine-driven pump replaced hand pump operation of the undercarriage retracting mechanism, and a de Havilland two-speed, 3-blade propeller replaced the original fixed pitch 2-blade unit from the 78th aircraft onwards. Powerplant for the first Mk Is was the 1030 hp R-R Merlin II, which gave way to the Merlin III from the 175th airframe. Of similar power, this engine could take either de Havilland or Rotol propellers, supplies of the latter becoming available in 1939.

The first of the many - K5054 was the prototype Spitfire, completed in March 1936. Here, the aircraft is still unpainted and has the original rudder balance design. Thousands of Spitfires were to be manufactured looking just like the prototype except for minor detail changes. (Vickers)

Vickers test pilot Jeffrey Quill taxies the prototype Spitfire out for a press demonstration at Eastleigh, 4 June 1936. (Flight)

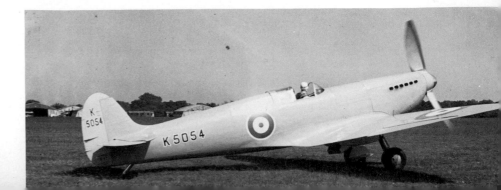

Wrecked but repairable, Mk I K9923, LZ-H of No. 66 Squadron awaits attention, most probably at No. 1 Civilian Repair Unit at Cowley, Oxfordshire. The coding dates the photograph as not earlier than September 1939, when No. 66's code letters were changed from RB to LZ. (Via Bruce Robertson)

The first Auxiliary Air Force squadron to receive Spitfires was No. 602 (City of Glasgow). This view of a 'B' Flight machine shows the half white half black (Night) underside paint scheme introduced in 1939, the early tall radio mast and the flame damping strip on the front fuselage. Under the windshield is the squadron badge, the coat of arms of Glasgow. (Flight)

Cowling Development

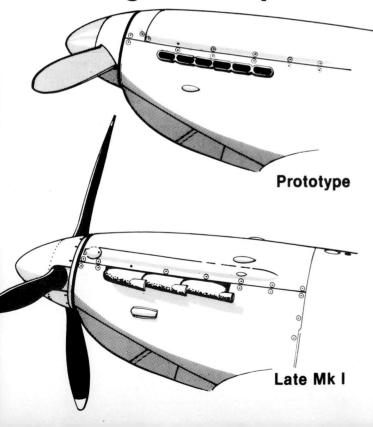

Prototype

Late Mk I

Spitfire Development

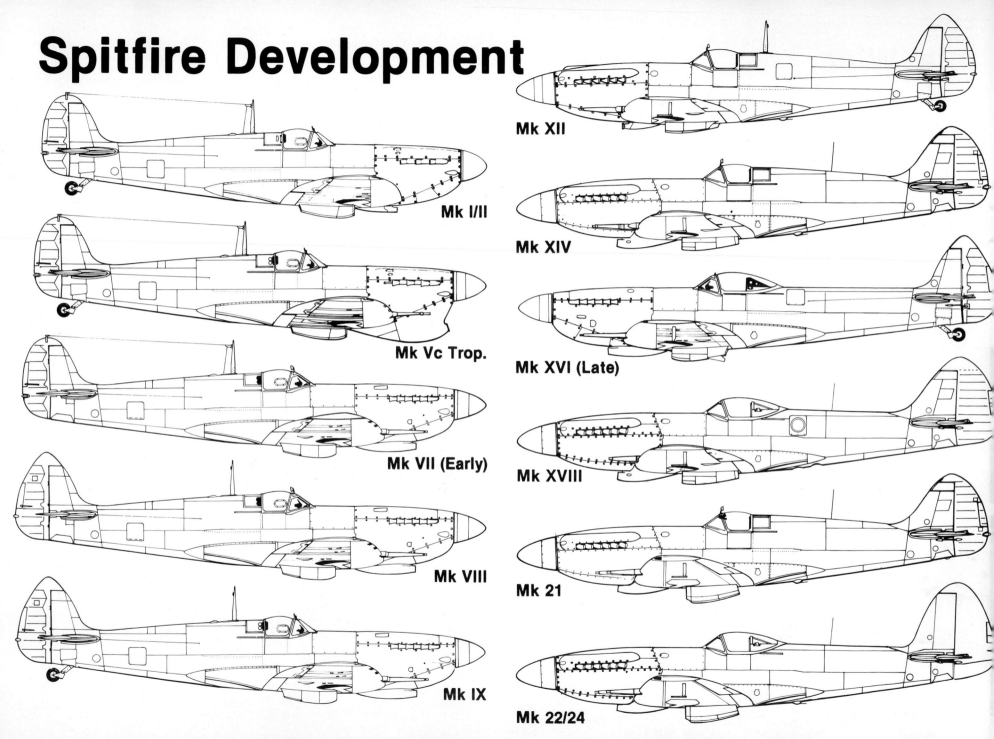

Mk I/II

Mk Vc Trop.

Mk VII (Early)

Mk VIII

Mk IX

Mk XII

Mk XIV

Mk XVI (Late)

Mk XVIII

Mk 21

Mk 22/24

'a' Wing

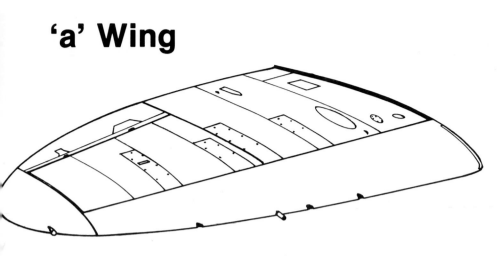

Armorers at work on another No. 602 Spitfire Mk I, this time an aircraft of 'A' Flight. Notice the scuffing of the wing root paint and the yellow gas detector patch. This and the previous photograph were probably taken at the squadron's home station, Abbotsinch, although four other bases were used at various times prior to August 1940. (Flight)

This unidentified Spitfire Mk Ia has been set up for test firing its guns. This was a part of the preservice testing of each new aircraft, and checked the operation of the electrical circuits and the bore-sighting of the guns. (Flight)

The same airplane during a firing test. The blurred objects below the wing are empty shell casings and belt links. In the air, the smoke seen here would not be apparent. (Flight)

Spitfire Mk I

Specifications

Dimensions: Span 36 ft. 10 in. length 29 ft. 11 in.; height 12 ft. 7¾ in.; wing area 242 sq. ft.
Weight: Normal loaded 6,200 lb.; wing loading 26 lb. per sq. ft.
Performance: Maximum speed 362 m.p.h.; rate of climb 2,530 ft. per min. Time to 20,000 ft. 9.4 min.; ceiling 31,900 ft. Range (including take-off and 15 min. combat) 395 miles.
Armament: 'a' Wing standard.

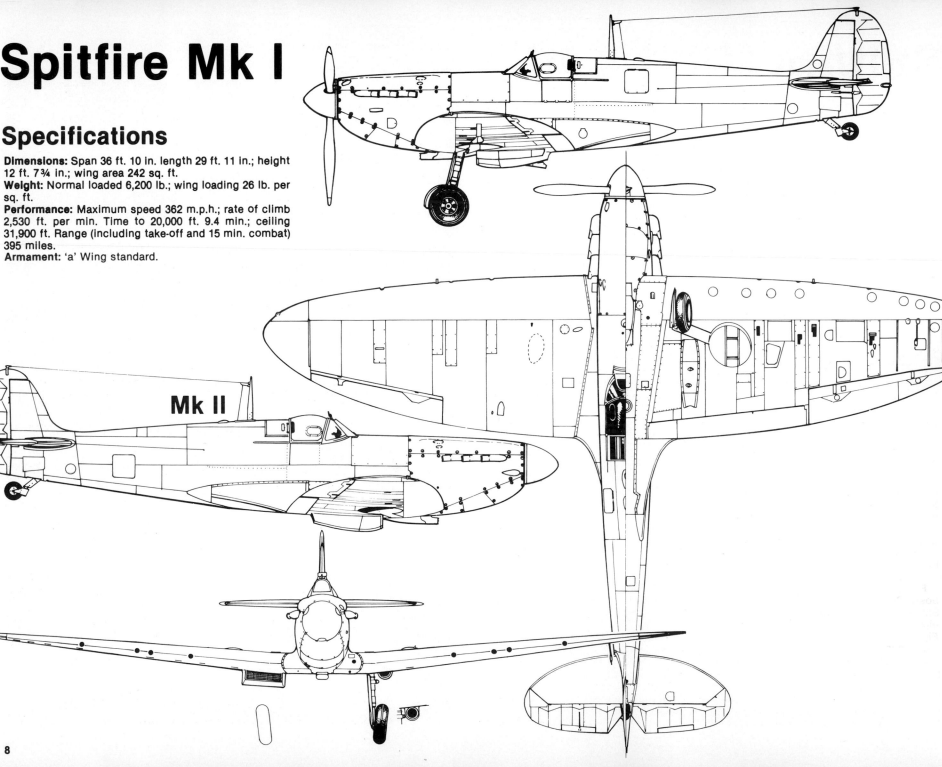

Spitfire Mk II & III

Incorporating the refinements of the later Mk Is, the Spitfire II was externally identical apart from a small blister fairing over the Coffman starter on the starboard side of the nose aft of the spinner. Powered by the Merlin XII of 1175 hp and using 100 rather than 87 octane fuel, it was built exclusively at a new plant at Castle Bromwich near Birmingham, the first airframe being completed in June 1940. The first 750 Mk IIs had 'a' wing armament, the remaining 170 the 'b' wing. Armor protection for the pilot totalled 73 lbs., the fuel tanks were self-sealing and a bullet-proof windshield was introduced during production, the latter also being retrofitted to Mk Is.

A number of experiments conducted with Mk IIs were aimed at boosting the Spitfire's normal range of 395 miles as, having been designed as a homebased defense fighter with the smallest possible airframe, the aircraft had little room for extra fuel tankage internally. Consequently, various external fuel tank arrangements were tested, including a 40 gal. type faired into the wing leading edge. Nos. 66, 118 and 152 Squadrons used Mk IIs with these tanks for a few operations, although their adverse effect on handling, plus the fact that they were non-jettisonable in combat, caused them to be withdrawn in favor of the fuselage 'slipper' tank.

Mk IIs also became the first Spitfires to carry bombs - albeit of the non-lethal smoke marker variety - when at least 52 examples became Mk IICs, the suffix denoting a different duty from that of Mk IIa/b fighters rather than a change in wing armament. These machines were officially known as 'Sea Rescue Type E (Spitfire)' and carried a small dinghy and food supplies for dropping by parachute. Used by five squadrons, they were redesignated ASR Mk IIs in late 1942.

For its day the Spitfire carried the formidable 'a' wing armament of eight 0.303 in. Browning machine guns, weapons comparable to - and indeed adapted from - American .30 in. guns. But although the number of guns was exceptionally high and each had 300 rounds, the weight of fire was light, rifle-caliber ammunition lacking the destructive power of shell-firing cannon. Consequently in June 1939, some service Spitfires were fitted with two 20mm Hispano cannon. Initial operational use was disappointing, the guns invariably jamming after only a few round had been fired. The problem was eventually traced to faulty feed mechanisms, and henceforth cannon became an integral part of British fighter aircraft armament.

Fitting the cannon necessitated some redesign of the Spitfire wing, each drum-type magazine requiring a raised 'blister' over its bay; with the addition of four machine guns, this wing took the suffix 'b' and in common with other armament layouts, was added to the mark number to denote each such change.

Spitfires were blooded in action for the first time over Scotland on 16 October 1939, when Nos. 602 and 603 Squadrons, Auxiliary Air Force, scrambled sections from Grangemouth and Turnhouse respectively to intercept Ju 88s attacking shipping in the Firth of Forth. A confused melee resulted in the destruction of one enemy aircraft, the victim of Sqdn. Ldr. E.E. Stevens, leading Red Section, 603 Squadron.

Further actions took place as the Luftwaffe probed Britain's defenses prior to the proposed German invasion and by the spring of 1940, a further eight squadrons had received Spitfire: Nos. 64, 92, 152, 222, 234, 266, 610 and 616. On the morning of 1 July there were eight Spitfire squadrons with 128 aircraft based in south-east England as part of 11 Group, Fighter Command, with six in 10 Group (92 aircraft) charged mainly with defense of the west country, and five in 12 Group (72 aircraft) in the northeastern part of the country.

That the Spitfires, backed up by 458 Hurricanes, were enough to destroy the myth of Luftwaffe invincibility and so forge the first turning point of the war, is part of history. The series of engagements that constituted the Battle of Britain highlighted technical and tactical weakness on both sides. More evenly matched than they had ever been, the Messerschmitt pilots were occasionally able to exploit one drawback with the early Spitfires - the tendency for the engine to cut out as a result of carburetor flooding under

negative Gs, particularly when the stick was pushed hard forward. An expedient solution in combat was a half-roll and dive in order to keep the engine running. Later, diaphragm carburetors cured the problem completely but a temporary measure was the insertion of a restricter orifice which prevented fuel from being flung to the top of the carburetor and momentarily starving the engine.

Although it was represented by but a single example, N3297, the Mk III was important as the first significant redesign of the Spitfire. It differed from previous marks by having clipped wings, a strengthened fuselage with a retractable tailwheel, an internal bullet-proof windshield and 88 lbs. of armor plating. Two inches more forward rake was added to the strengthened undercarriage and the wheels were enclosed by doors when retracted. Used as a test bed, N3297 subsequently flew with different armament and radiator designs, and engines in the Merlin 60 and 61 series.

The Spitfire cockpit, showing the distinctive 'spade handle' control column grip with gun firing thumb button on the left. Stout locks are holding the 'stick' rigid in this view. (Via Bruce Robertson)

Adorned with appropriate initials and rank pennant below the windscreen, Mk II P7966 was the mount of Wing Commander Douglas Bader in the summer of 1941 when he led the Tangmere Wing. (P. Allonby)

Pictured at Tangmere early in 1941, Mk IIa P7753 was the usual aircraft of Flt. Lt. L. H. Casson. On charge to No. 616 Sqdn (despite the 'QJ' code of No. 92 Sqdn), the machine appears to have a dark outline to its fuselage roundel due to the use of orthochromatic film, (P. Allonby)

Spitfire Mk V

With the end of the daylight phase of the Battle of Britain, Fighter Command rested those squadrons that had borne the brunt of the fighting and prepared for an extended and equally grueling campaign of offensive operations across the Channel, which was to last until June 1944. Progressively equipped with Spitfires as the Hurricane was phased out, the day fighter squadrons maintained pressure on numerous targets in the occupied countries, within a broad framework of operations, the most important of which were given code names: **Rhubarb** - small scale attacks by fighters or fighter bombers; **Circus** -heavy escort to light bombers acting as bait to bring enemy fighters to battle; **Ramrod** -similar to a Circus but with the primary object of destroying the bombers' target; **Roadstead** - an attack by bombers under fighter escort on shipping targets; **Rodeo** - a straightforward fighter sweep over enemy territory; and **Ranger** - a freelance penetration of enemy airspace in squadron or wing strength aimed at wearing down the defenses.

Such operations were costly in both men and machines and although (until the advent of the Fw 190 in the autumn of 1941) Spitfire squadrons were able to hold their own against the Bf 109E and F, German fighters were only one of the hazards to be faced. Many Spitfires fell not in aerial combat but to ground fire of all calibers, ranging from rifle rounds to purpose-built flak guns. The victims, including experienced pilots such as Bob Stanford-Tuck and 'Paddy' Finucane, were sorely missed.

At the beginning of 1941, with the Spitfire equipping most operational fighter squadrons, every effort was made behind the scenes to ensure that it remained at least equal to its Luftwaffe adversaries. Nonetheless, it was obviously undesirable to disrupt production by introducing any radical design changes. Thus, in February, No. 92 Squadron was the first to receive examples of the interim Mk V, followed by No. 91 in March. These machines were part of the initial order for 1000 Mk Vs.

Externally similar to preceeding variants, the Mk V was a Mk I/II airframe with longerons strengthened to take a Merlin 45 powerplant combat-rated at 1470 hp. By June 1941, production of the Mk Va with machine gun armament was terminated in favor of the Vb, which had a mixed armament of 20mm cannon and 0.303 in. MGs.

Early Vb aircraft had the full span wings of the Mks I and II, although to improve low altitude performance, clipped wings of 30 ft. 6 in. span were introduced later. Numerous detail improvement were made to the Mk V throughout its production life at both manufacturer and service levels, the most significant for the former being a jettisonable cockpit canopy with more bulbous contours, replacement of metal-covered ailerons and the fitting of 'fishtail' flame-damping exhaust stubs.

By September 1941, 27 RAF squadrons were flying the Mk Vb and a few the Va; by December this figure had risen to 46 plus the first two American 'Eagle' squadrons. Output had passed the 1700 mark by early 1942 and the first Westland-built machine flew in January to push the total for the year to more than 3300. By June 1942, there were 59 UK-based fighter squadrons with Mk Vs, plus seven in the Mediterranean; two months later no fewer than 42 Spitfire Mk V units were available to cover the landings at Dieppe.

As the most numerous of all Spitfire variants, the Mk V was eventually to equip more than 100 RAF squadrons, be sold to nine foreign governments and fly operationally in the hands of nationals of over a dozen countries; it was engaged on every battle front where RAF or Allied air forces were committed.

As the threat of an invasion of England receded, the first of those far-flung battle fronts was the Mediterranean where, by the spring of 1942, defense of the island of Malta was becoming critical. Only Spitfires could meet the German fighters on equal terms, and in consequence the first tropicalized Mk Vs were dispatched to Malta by aircraft carrier.

With a large and unmistakeable under-nose fairing over the Vokes Multi-Vee filter for the carburetor air intake, the Mk Vc also had enlarged oil and radiator intakes for more effective cooling in tropical and desert climates. To improve range, three sizes of fuselage slipper tanks - 30 gal. for short range, 90 gal. for long range and 170 gal. for ferrying - could be fitted to belly attachment lugs.

The Mk V was built to take various engines, including the Merlin 45 (F Mk Va); 45 or 46 (F Mk Vb); 45, 46, 50, 50A, 55 or 56 (F Mk Vc) and Merlin 45M, 50M or 55M (LF Mk Vb). The 'c' suffix denoted a new wing fitted with either four cannon or two cannon plus four MGs or eight MGs. The landing gear had two inches more forward rake on strengthened units, as tested on the Mk III. A number of the Mk Vc aircraft sent to Malta had four cannon wings, although the second pair of guns was invariably removed due to a shortage of ammunition on the island, and because two cannon were not only found to be adequate in combat but also enabled the aircraft to climb faster. Four-cannon Mk Vs were subsequently used in action.

While the great majority of Mk Vs intended for overseas use were fitted with the Vokes filter fairing, a smaller, more streamlined fitting was developed by No. 103 Maintenance Unit at Aboukir, Egypt. Five machines modified by this same unit formed the 'Special Performance Flight' for the interception of very high altitude Ju 86 reconnaissance aircraft, the Mk Vs with clipped wings successfully catching enemy aircraft at heights of 40,000 ft. One example was later fitted with a Merlin 61 with a four-bladed propeller and multiple exhaust stacks, although it was by no means the only Mk V so modified in a theatre that saw much expedient interchanging of parts during repairs and overhauls.

The Spitfire was widely used as a fighter-bomber in the Mediterranean, Mk Vs carrying two 250 lbs. bombs on wing racks and up to 500 lbs. on a fuselage centerline carrier. Engines more suited to low level operations, such as the Merlin 45M, 50M or 55M, were fitted, these powerplants having negative G carburetors and fuel de-aerators. In the LF Mk V, these and other modifications gave an increased climb rate of 7000 ft. per minute and 9 mph more speed at heights below 4-5,000 ft.

In flight during the summer of 1941, R6923/QJ-S of No. 92 Sqdn is seen with the CO, Squadron Leader Jimmy Rankin, at the controls. One of the original cannon-armed Spitfire Is issued to No. 19 Sqdn during 1940, R6923 was brought up to Mk V standard and issued to No. 92 early in 1941. The 'East India Squadron' title appears forward of the windshield, with 'Sheila' painted diagonally below it. Some retouching of the dark green camouflage color is evident. (Imperial War Museum)

Probably photographed during the autumn of 1941 at Gravesend in Kent, these Mk Vb Spitfires are from No. 72 Sqdn, which then formed part of the Biggin Hill Wing. The unit used Gravesend - Biggin Hill's satellite field - during July and was based there again from September 1941 to March 1942. (Via Robertson)

(Above right) Second of the Polish fighter squadrons to be formed in the UK, No. 303 drew its personnel from Nos. 111 'Koscluszko' and 112 'Warsaw' Fighter Squadrons, Polish Air Force. Here, a pilot prepares for a sortie in Mk Vb AR335, typically marked with both the Polish flash and Kosciuszko squadron badge. (Gen. Sikorsky Historical Institute)

The first Australian fighter squadron to form in the UK was No. 452, in April 1941. Moving to Redhill in October, its aircraft included AD537/UD-R, pictured here with LAC D. Keeble and Sgt. Ken Bassett. (Frank F. Smith)

Mk V Canopy

(external armor)

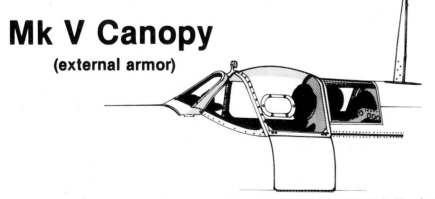

The second RAAF Squadron was No. 457. It received the Spitfire Mk Vb in March 1942 and also moved to Redhill, in May. Identifiable only by its last two serial digits, '05', this aircraft makes a dispersal point study that was repeated thousands of times all over the world during the war. (F.F. Smith)

Good detail view of a Mk Vb at the moment of 'Chocks away'. (Vickers)

Among the many pilots lost during low-level fighter sweeps over France was the famous ace Robert Stanford-Tuck, brought down by groundfire. This view of Tuck's Mk Vb shows his kill tally and the wood Jablo propeller, which has shattered on impact. This aircraft was later retrieved for salvage. (Bundesarchiv)

(Below Left) Ignominiously dumped, these three Spitfires were early examples of the vast numbers of Allied aircraft to fall on continental Europe during the war years. In the foreground is a Mk Vb of No. 234 Sqdn, then another Vb of No. 306, (possibly AB364/UZ-A) and finally the Mk V flown by Robert Stanford-Tuck, coded 'RS-T' and displaying his tally of 29 kills on the fuel tank cover. (Bundesarchiv)

Down on a French beach, Mk Vb AA837, late of No. 501 (County of Gloucester) Squadron has a line attached to its tailwheel leg in preparation for dragging away, although subsequent pictures of the incident show that this was not accomplished before the tide came in! (Bundesarchiv)

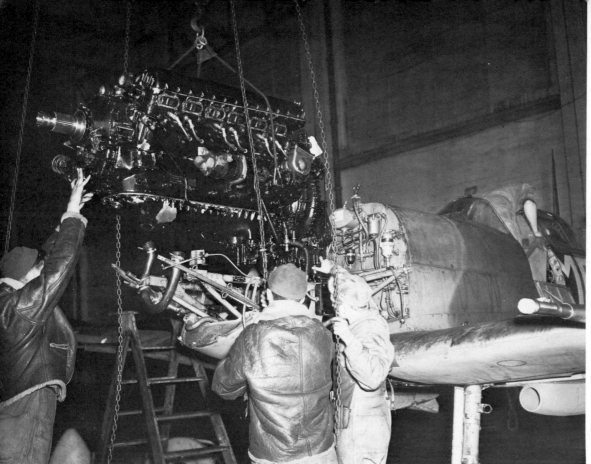

Having its radio serviced and fuel tanks replenished, this Mk Vb is seen while on strength with the 308th FS, 31st FG during operations from the UK between June and October 1942; code letters HL-U. (Aeroplane Monthly)

(Above Left) If the April 1943 dating of this photo is correct, then not only an engine is about to be changed, but also the Spitfire. April was the month that the 336th FS went operational on P-47s, the last 4th FG squadron to do so, at Debden, Essex. The 'MD' codes seen on this Spitfire Vb would also change, to 'VF' on the P-47 Thunderbolts. (USAF)

Some of the 143 Mk Vbs delivered to the Russians await collection by their new owners from a depot in the Persian Gulf, probably Abadan. Marked with black-outlined red stars, the group of aircraft seen here includes EP495. (IWM)

'b' Wing

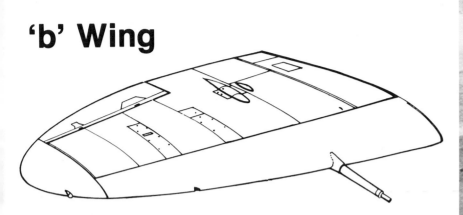

New film goes into the wing root gun camera of a Mk Vb of No. 303 Squadron in a sand-bagged dispersal at Northolt. The machine's Polish pilot has at least seven victories chalked up. (Gen. Sikorsky Historical Institute)

An echelon formation of Mk Vbs from No. 81 Squadron seen in the summer of 1942, when it was part of the Hornchurch Wing. Most aircraft have serials in the 'BM' range, FL-J being BM378 and right at the rear, BM461 is 'A'. (IWM)

A striking air-to-air view of a Mk Vb, EN821/SN-M of No. 243 Sqdn, a unit reformed in the UK after flying Brewster Buffaloes against the Japanese. Remaining in Britain for about three months before transferring to Algeria in December 1942, No. 243 flew Spitfires until disbanding in Italy in October 1944.

(Below Left) No. 340 Sqdn, the first Free French fighter unit formed in the RAF, taxies out for take off in its Mk Vbs. (ECPA)

A Polish pilot leaps from his Spitfire after an obviously successful sortie. The squadron is No. 302, the aircraft Mk Vb W3902/WX-T. (Gen. Sikorsky Historical Institute)

The third RAAF Spitfire squadron in the Pacific area, No. 79 was formed in July 1943 and participated in an island-hopping campaign that began on Goodenough Island and ended in Borneo. En route it used Horn Island, one of the group of Thursday Islands off Australia's Cape York Peninsula, where Mk Vc JG807/UP-P is seen landing in 1943. (F.F. Smith)

Formed in Australia, No. 451 Sqdn operated in North Africa and Italy until the end of 1944. August 1943 saw the unit at El Daba, where these five Mk Vc fighters were photographed. In the foreground is LZ943, with EF655/A next in line; clearly visible on the nearest machine is the tailplane-to-fuselage aerial for IFF equipment. (F.F. Smith)

Spitfire Mk Vb ER810 shows the major recognition points of the tropicalized Spitfires intended for service in the Mediterranean. The most noticeable is the deep chin fairing for the Vokes tropical air filter. Although causing some drop in speed, this filter enabled engines to run far longer in dusty conditions before being replaced. Note the piping going from the rear exhaust stack into the cowling. This delivered hot air for heating the guns at high altitudes. (Vickers)

A Spitfire Vb of No. 310 (Czech) Sqdn. This represents the typical mid-war appearance of the Spitfire with Type 'C' roundels, Light Grey codes, Sky fuselage band and spinner and the new Ocean Grey, Dark Green and Medium Sea Grey camouflage. (Dusan Mikolas)

Spitfire Mk Vb

Specifications

Dimensions: "B" Wing 36 ft. 10 in. length 29 ft. 11 in.; height 9 ft. 11 in.; wing area 242 sq. ft.

Weights: Empty 5,065 lb. Normal load 6,750 lb. Maximum 6,710 lb., bomb load was limited to 500 lb. for operations.

Performance: Maximum speed 369 m.p.h. at 19,500 ft. Normal cruising 272 m.p.h. at 5,000 ft. Rate of climb 4,750 ft. per min. Service ceiling 36,200 ft. Absolute ceiling 36,700 ft. Stalling speed (at 6,400 lb. weight) 78 m.p.h. (flaps up), 70 m.p.h. (flaps down)

Armament: 'b' Wing standard, some 'a' or 'c'

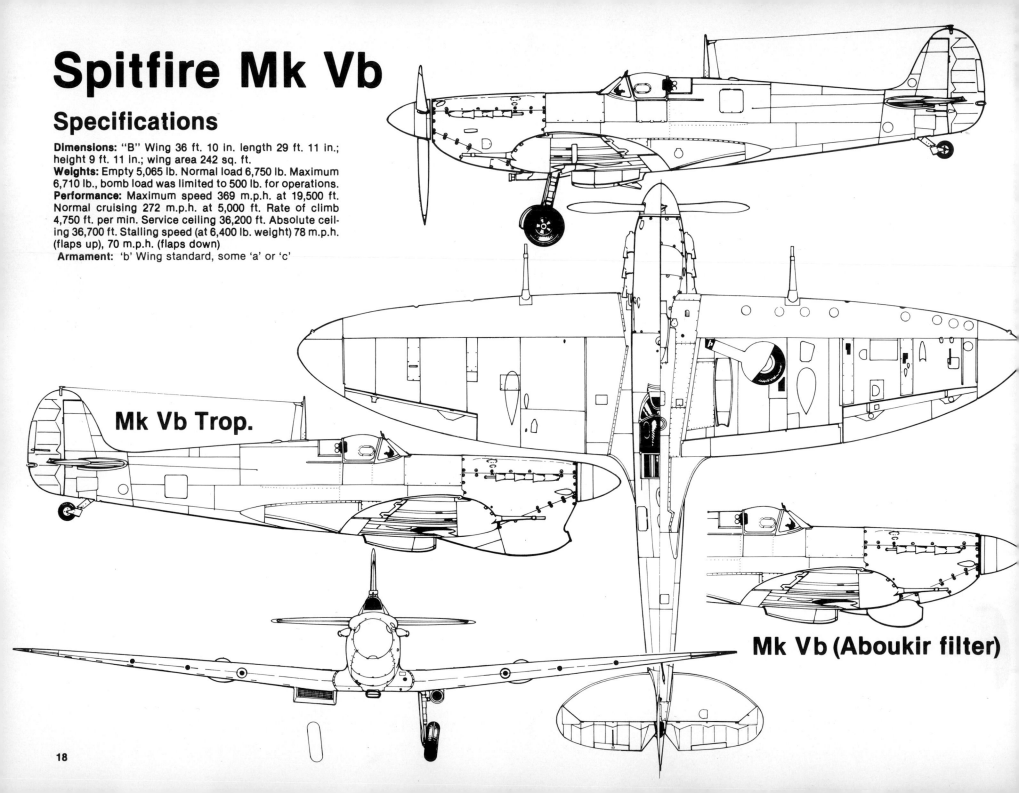

Mk Vb Trop.

Mk Vb (Aboukir filter)

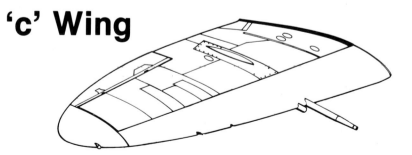

Still bearing the US flag marking applied for the North African landings, this Spitfire Vc is seen at a repair depot after being shot down in central Tunisia early in 1943. A machine of the 5th FS, 52nd FG. (USAF)

(Above Left) In Dec. 1942, Brig. Gen. Jimmy Doolittle visited Tafaraoui, Algeria, home of the 31st FG, and borrowed a Spitfire Vc of the 308th Squadron for a short flight. This starboard side view of the machine he used (coded HL-M) shows the 'Lobo' marking which appeared only on this side, and the black shadows to the code letters. (USAF)

Some Mediterranean maintenance units handled Spitfires in almost production line quantities, although the resulting machines were often far from new. (ECPA)

'c' Wing

Over the Adriatic en route to a target in Italy, this heavily armed Mk Vc fighter bomber of No. 2 Squadron SAAF is fitted with four wing cannon and carries a 500 lb. bomb on the centerline rack. Sporting No. 2's 'Flying Cheetah' emblem on the rudder, this machine has had its serial digits overpainted, leaving only the prefix letters 'JK'. (Imperial War Museum)

Interesting view of Mk Vs at a Mediterranean depot, probably Blida, on being transferred to French Air Force control. The machine being towed appears to have PRU type roundels and fin flash with white rear fuselage band and spinner, an unusual combination on this camouflage finish. (ECPA)

(Above Right) Spitfire Vc LZ820 of the 4th FS, 52nd FG crash-landed at Borgotaro, Italy on 19 December 1943, apparently after running out of fuel in the company of two other Spitfires which also put down there. Fitted with a Merlin 61 with multiple exhaust manifolds and three-blade propeller the aircraft bears the name 'Pauline' on the nose and 'Capt. Kelly' forward of the insignia. The machine almost certainly retains the Vokes filter fairing under the nose. (P. Guerra via Interinfo)

This Mediterranean airfield shows a Mk Vc in USAAF service, bearing non-standard codes. This Spitfire was flown by Fred Murray Dean, the Commanding Officer of 31 FG, and bears his initials: FMD. This is one of the few U.S. aircraft to show the adoption of the British practice of a CO using his initials on his aircraft in place of squadron or group codes. (USAF Museum via R. Warren)

Mk V Canopy
(internal armor)

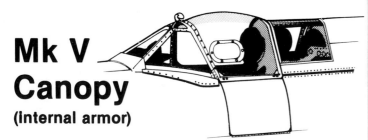

Languishing in a dump after the war, this Turkish Air Force Mk Vc has a Mk IX-type pointed rudder, probably taken from one of the latter variants supplied after the end of WWII. Previously Spitfire Vs had carried the star and crescent insignia on the rudder. (Turkish Air Force)

Early Photo Reconnaissance Spitfires

Development of the early photographic reconnaissance Spitfires was not directly related to that of the fighter variants, but is included here to retain the chronological sequence. Broadly speaking, there were four marks (A-D) of PR Spitfires before the Mk V, although their designations referred to equipment changes on the same airframe. They were identified as follows: **PR Type A** - two Mk IIs fitted with wing cameras; **Type B** -retrospective designations of the Type A machines fitted with a 29 gal. internal fuel tank; **Type C** (Also known as the PR Mk I and III) - initially these were the same Mk IIs, converted to take the rear fuselage fuel tank and wing and fuselage cameras, but this designation also applied to other conversions from Mks I and V airframes, one of which had the 'D' wing with internal fuel to boost range to 2000 miles.

Several modifications were made to the **Type D** (PR Mk III) - the wings had 66.5 gal. fuel tanks on each side and two F.8 and F.24 cameras were mounted in the fuselage in tandem to give overlapping photographs, wing cameras and the extra fuselage fuel tank being dispensed with. Total fuel carried was 218 gals. Cockpit heating was improved, the oxygen supply was increased and additional oil was housed in a 14 gal. port wing tank. Two aircraft were built to Type D standard, the powerplant in both cases being the Merlin III.

Apart from the installation of a Merlin 45, the Spitfire PR Mk IV was identical to the two Type D PR Mk IIIs. Standardization of camera fittings was as follows: 'W fitting' - two F.8 cameras with 20 in. focal length lens, 'S fitting' - two F.24 cameras with 14 in. lens, and 'Y fitting' - two F.52 cameras with 36 in. lens.

The 229 PR IVs were all offset from Mk Va/b orders. No armament was fitted, wing leading edges housing 66.5 gal. fuel tanks to give a total of 218 gallons. Other standard equipment included a 'K' type dinghy, 1.5 gals. of drinking water and TR 1133 r/t set. The PR Mk IV was fitted with the Aboukir filter, and saw widespread service.

The designation PR Mk V was initially applied to 15 Mk V conversions fitted with the Merlin 45 and Type C camera installation. It was subsequently changed to PR Mk IV to avoid confusion with standard Mk V fighters.

The Spitfire PR Mk VII (also referred to as the type G) was the first armed PR Spitfire. Fitted with two F.24 vertical cameras in the rear fuselage and the 29 gal. fuel tank below the seat, the PR Mk VII featured a bulletproof shield, reflector gunsight, armor, and teardrop blisters in the cockpit canopy. 45 PR Mk VIIs were produced by Heston in 1941-42, converted from standard Mk I fighters.

Above and below: A PR Mk IV, BP904 of No. 2 Photographic Reconnaissance Unit, in North Africa in 1943. Note the frameless windshield and 'tear drop' bulged canopy sides to give the pilot maximum possible vision. (F.F. Smith)

PR Tear Drop Hood

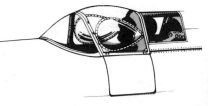

21

Spitfire HF Mk VI

Based on the Mk V airframe, the HF Mk VI was the first Spitfire specifically intended for high altitude combat, rather than reconnaissance duties. Fitted with a pressurized cockpit and powered by a Merlin 47 of 1415 hp, it had increased span 'c' wings of 40 ft. 2 in. Although intended for use in England, No. 124 Sqdn receiving its first example in February 1941, five were shipped to the Middle East to replace the Special Performance Flight Mk Vs.

In the event, the Mk VI's performance fell short of expectations and only 97 were completed; it did not prove as good as the modified SPF Mk Vs overseas, being unable to reach Ju 86P-2 flights then operating at 50,000 ft. The most serious drawback was the fact that the canopy had to be locked down to allow pressurization and was not intended to be opened in flight, although it could be jettisoned in an emergency.

Relegated to second-line and training duties, the majority of Mk VIs had their pointed wingtips replaced by standard tips and armament removed.

Spitfire Mk VII

Development of the Merlin-engined Spitfires reached a peak in the Mks VII and VIII, both of which incorporated considerable design changes. The pressurized Mk VII was the first variant to have rectangular radiator air intakes of similar section on each wing underside rather than a circular section oil cooler that had given the Spitfire its distinct asymmetrical appearance from head-on. This change was the result of a redesigned engine cooling system for the Merlin 61, 64 or 71 with multi-ejector exhaust manifolds. Both air inscoops contained radiators, that on the starboard side being for the supercharger intercooler, that on the port for the oil cooler.

To accommodate longer engine mounts, the fuselage of the Mk VII was stretched to 31 ft. 3.5 in. with the early rounded rudder, 31 ft. 6 in. with the broad chord rudder. A retractable tailwheel was also fitted. Pressurization was a later version of the system fitted to the HF Mk VI, with a similar location but now the advantage of a sliding cockpit canopy. Extended tips were fitted to the 'c' type wings, which had reduced span ailerons and two leading edge 14 gal. fuel tanks. In high altitude form, the aircraft attained a maximum speed of 416 mph at 44,000 ft. Thus configured the Mk VII was powered by a 1250 hp Merlin 71, medium altitude fighters having either the 1565 hp Merlin 61 or 1710 hp Merlin 64.

The first special high-altitude version of the Spitfire, the HF Mk VI served with eight squadrons, No. 124 being one of the first. Seen at Debden in July 1942 is BR579/ON-H, with extended wingtips and the cabin pressure air intake below the exhausts. (IWM)

Spitfire PR Mk X

As the photographic reconnaissance equivalent of the Mk VII fighter, the PR X was generally similar, although the wing carried two leading edge tanks of 66.5 gal. each instead of armament. Only 16 aircraft were built and issued to two RAF PR units in May 1944 - after service introduction of the Mk XI. As maintenance of such a limited production variant proved to be difficult and the pressure cabin gave visibility problems, the type was withdrawn in September 1945.

An unidentified very early Spitfire Mk VII, showing the features of this version. Note the extended wing tips, symmetrical underwing radiators, bulge for the Coffman starter and just behind it, the long intake for the cabin air compressor. Later Mk VIIs were fitted with the broader pointed rudder. (Vickers)

Significantly different in external appearance from other Merlin marks, the Spitfire Mk VII had a double-glazed sliding canopy (compared to a fixed canopy on the Mk VI, which it resembled from a distance) and matched radiator air scoops under the wings which gave a symmetrical appearance when seen head-on. This example, in the MD100 - 146 production batch, belonged to No. 131 Sqdn in the autumn of 1944. The Mk VII was the last Spitfire variant to be used in Europe by No. 131, which left for India in November. (Via B. Robertson)

Spitfire Mk VIII

Designed before the Mk IX, but following it into service because its radical design changes would have meant production delays when time was of the essence, the Spitfire Mk VIII was an unpressurized Mk VII. Powered by the Merlin 61, 63 or 63A in standard fighter form, Merlin 66 in LF form and Merlin 70 for high altitude work, it incorporated the Vokes Aero-Vee filter in a streamlined under-nose fairing. All Mk VIIIs were built for overseas use and, fitted with the 'c' wing developed for the Mk VII, were stressed to carry up to 1000 lb. of bombs on wing and center section racks. Early machines had the pointed wingtips of the Mk VII, although standard wingtips were subsequently fitted.

The Mk VIII saw widespread use in the Mediterranean and Far Eastern theatres, the USAAF and RAAF as well as the RAF accepting large numbers. Post war, a single Mk VIII became the prototype Spitfire Trainer with the existing cockpit moved forward 13.5 in. to make room for a second cockpit set higher and enclosed by a bubble canopy. Full instrumentation was provided in both positions and altered CG compensated for by revising the fuel system. Production trainers were Mk IX airframes.

JF275 shows the appearance of early Mk VIII fighters. The major difference from the Mk VII was the lack of a pressurized cockpit. Like the Mk VII, later Mk VIIIs had the pointed broad rudder, but retained 'c' wing armament. (Vickers)

A Spitfire HF VIII with extended wingtips runs up at a 308th FS dispersal, probably at San Severo, Italy, spring 1944. (Via C. F. Shores)

Mk VIII A58-300 of No. 54 Sqdn, dispersed at Darwin, Northern Territory in 1944, takes on fuel. Painting the individual aircraft letter in white was a common practice with this unit. (F.F. Smith)

Mk VIII 'c' Wing (extended)

No. 452 Squadron RAAF seen flying its Mk VIIIs from Morotai, Netherlands East Indies, 30 December 1944. All aircraft carry the distinctive 'Ace of Spades' marking of No. 80 Fighter Wing on their rudders, although only the nearest machine, A58-516, that flown by the flight commander, has its codes aft of the roundel. (F.F. Smith)

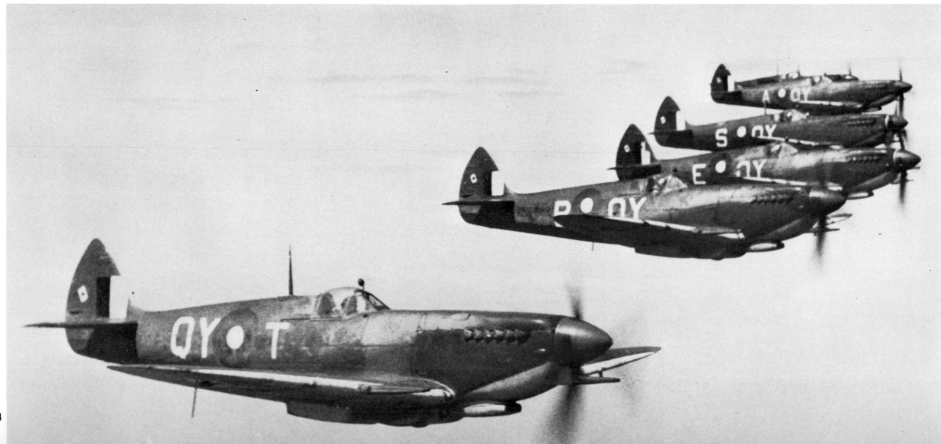

Arriving in India in May 1942, No. 607 (County of Durham) Sqdn was one of the first RAF fighter units in the Far East to get Spitfires when Mk Vs were received that September. Mk VIIIs came along in March 1944 and it was with these that No. 607 finished the war - and its operational life, being disbanded at Mingaladon on 19 August 1945. This photograph shows Air Vice-Marshal C. A. Bouchier CB, CBE, DFC, paying the squadron a surprise visit for a short farewell speech that day. Greeting him is Fl. Lt. D. E. Nicholson, who carried out this auxiliary squadron's last sortie of the war. (Via B. Robertson)

Tail Development

Early Mk VIII

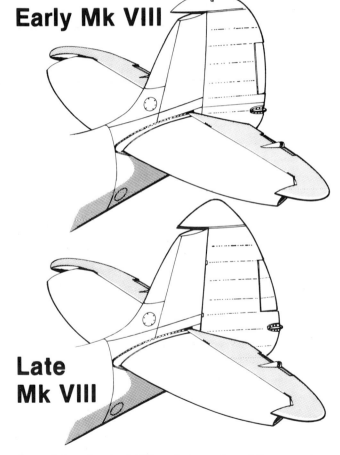

Late Mk VIII

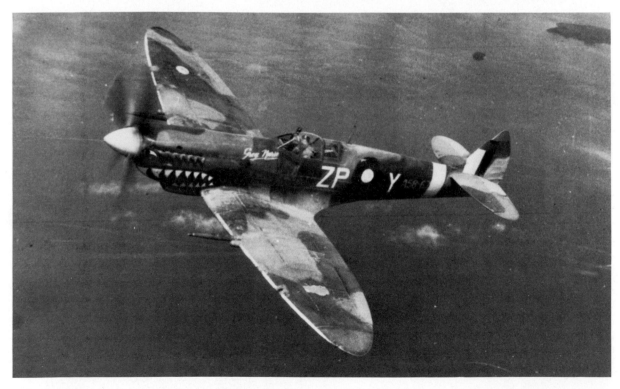

One of the classic Spitfire photographs of the war shows A58-672, the Mk VIII flown by Wing Commander Glen Cooper of 457 Sqdn RAAF, banking of the coast of Morotai in 1945. Decorated with appropriate sharkmouths, the 'Grey Nurse' Squadron's Spitfires were unmistakable. (F.F. Smith)

Spitfire Mk IX

With the appearance of the Fw 190 on the Channel coast late in 1941, Fighter Command faced a serious dilemma. The new German fighter was clearly superior to the Spitfire Mk V on nearly every count (a fact soberingly verified in June 1942 when an Fw 190A-3 was flown into RAF Pembey in Wales and thoroughly tested). Thus the need for an improved Spitfire became paramount. It was felt however, that introduction of a radically-changed variant would take too long and disrupt production and operations at a difficult time. Fortunately an expedient solution was on hand in the form of an interim version, basically a more powerful Mk V which could be ready for squadron service with the miniumum delay. This was the Mk IX, a superb fighting machine not only able to match the Fw 190 but considered by many to be the finest Spitfire of all.

Installation of the Merlin 61 engine of 1565 hp in the basic Mk Vb airframe was undertaken by Supermarine at Castle Bromwich as supplies became available. The first F Mk IXs were in operational service by July 1942. Armament of the Mk IX was initially that of the 'b' and 'c' type wings, pending the new 'e' or 'Universal' wing with 4 x 20mm Hispano cannon or two cannon and two 0.5 in. Browning machine guns, which was fitted to later series aircraft.

The 'e' wing was distinguishable from the 'c' wing by the cannon position, each weapon being mounted in the outer bay when only two were fitted, as the wing had shown a tendency to fail when bomb racks were also fitted. Buckling occurred on a number of occasions at the point where the rack was attached to the underside of the cannon bay in use.

Early production Mk IXs retained the rounded fin and rudder tip of the Mk V although later machines had a broad-chord pointed-tipped rudder. This feature, together with a clear view 'bubble' canopy made late Mk IXs identical to the Mk XVI. Operational Mk IXs were the first to carry the distinctive 50 gal. cylindrical drop tank on the fuselage rack, and a larger forward fuel tank with 95 gal. in the nose, two 18 gal. fabric fuel cells in the wings and a 72 gal. fuselage tank behind the pilot's seat gave a total capacity of 253 gallons.

Production of the Mk IX was second only to that of the Mk V, reaching 5,665. No. 64 Squadron was the first RAF unit to receive it and by D-Day there were 34 squadrons to support the invasion, plus 22 in England as part of Air Defence Great Britain (ADGB), as Fighter Command had been known since 15 November 1943. As well as fighter duties, Mk IXs carried out a considerable number of ground attack sorties during the invasion period, armed with a maximum 1000 lbs. of bombs on wing and fuselage racks.

Three main sub variants of the Mk IX saw service: F Mk IX (1565 hp Merlin 61 or 1650 hp Merlin 63); LF Mk IX (1580 hp Merlin 66) and HF Mk IX (1475 hp Merlin 70).

As noted, Mk IX production provided the 20 Spitfire Trainer conversions, all of which were sold to overseas governments post war. Internal changes were made to fuel capacity, there being no leading edge tanks and the original fixed tailwheel was replaced by a retractable unit. Large numbers of Mk IX fighters went overseas both during and after the war, the cost of a single example at 1943 prices being £45,000, or approximately $180,000.

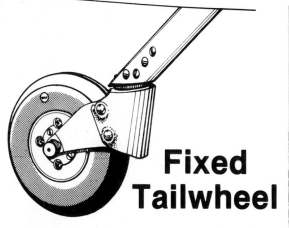

Fixed Tailwheel

In November 1944, this base in southern Italy held a variety of Allied aircraft, including representative machines from at least five Spitfire squadrons: second from left is Mk Vc LZ836/SW-D of No. 253 Sqdn; another Mk Vc of this unit stands next to a Mk IX of No. 73 Sqdn with a distinctive blue and yellow fuselage flash and no spinner in the center of the photograph. Also apparent is a Mk IX (LK-W) and two Mk Vcs from No. 87 Sqdn, a Mk VIII (AN-B) of No. 417 Sqdn and a Vc from No. 249 Sqdn, probably JL346/GL-F. At the extreme left is a Mk V in the EP65- serial range fitted with a Merlin 61 engine and painted in the markings of the Italian Co-Belligerent Air Force with unusual white wing bands. (IWM)

Virtually the whole of No. 485 Squadron was at Bovingdon when this photograph was taken on 30 March 1944, the unit having recently re-equipped with the Mk IXb. That month the squadron flew an armament practice camp, probably from Bovingdon, which was then non-operational and functioning as a B-17 Combat Crew Replacement Center, AAF Station 112. Identifiable Spitfires here include MK347/P; MK249/J; MK293/A; MK202/S and MK246/M, all with the original rounded vertical tail surfaces, while a solitary aircraft has the later pointed rudder. (USAF)

A Spitfire IX in the RK serial block being moved to a final assembly point at the Castle Bromwich plant. The 82 gal. fuel tank has yet to be installed in the bay forward of the windshield and much of the cockpit equipment, including the seat, would still be missing at this stage. Points of interest include the integral aft section of the wing root fillet and the way the electrical fitting is 'built out' to the curve of the root fairing. (Vickers)

Absorbing almost the entire complement of No. 167 Sqdn personnel, No. 322 Sqdn formed at Hornchurch on 12 June 1943 as an all-Dutch fighter unit. Moving to native soil on 31 December 1944, it flew initially from Woensdrecht, where this photograph was probably taken. It shows Mk IXs with the unit's newly applied code letters '3W', aircraft 'K', 'D', and 'F' being visible. (L.L. Peeters)

During operations to liberate Italy, No. 92 squadron made a practice of using numbers instead of letters to identify individual aircraft. This Mk IX, EN446, was QJ-1 at Grottaglie at the start of the campaign in September 1943. (F.F. Smith)

(Below Right) Probably at Bazenville, France, with the invasion of Europe barely a week old, this photograph shows hectic activity to repair a Mk IX of No. 403 (Canadian) Sqdn. Men of an RAF advance salvage team support the wing while the cannon barrel provides a leverage point to help it off. Fracturing of the propeller blades indicates Jablo wood composite construction. (IWM)

This Mk IXc, 'DU-L' of No. 312 (Czech) Sqdn, is the subject of our cover painting. These full top and bottom D-Day invasion stripes were very conspicuous, and were removed from the upper surfaces fairly quickly. (Dusan Mikolas)

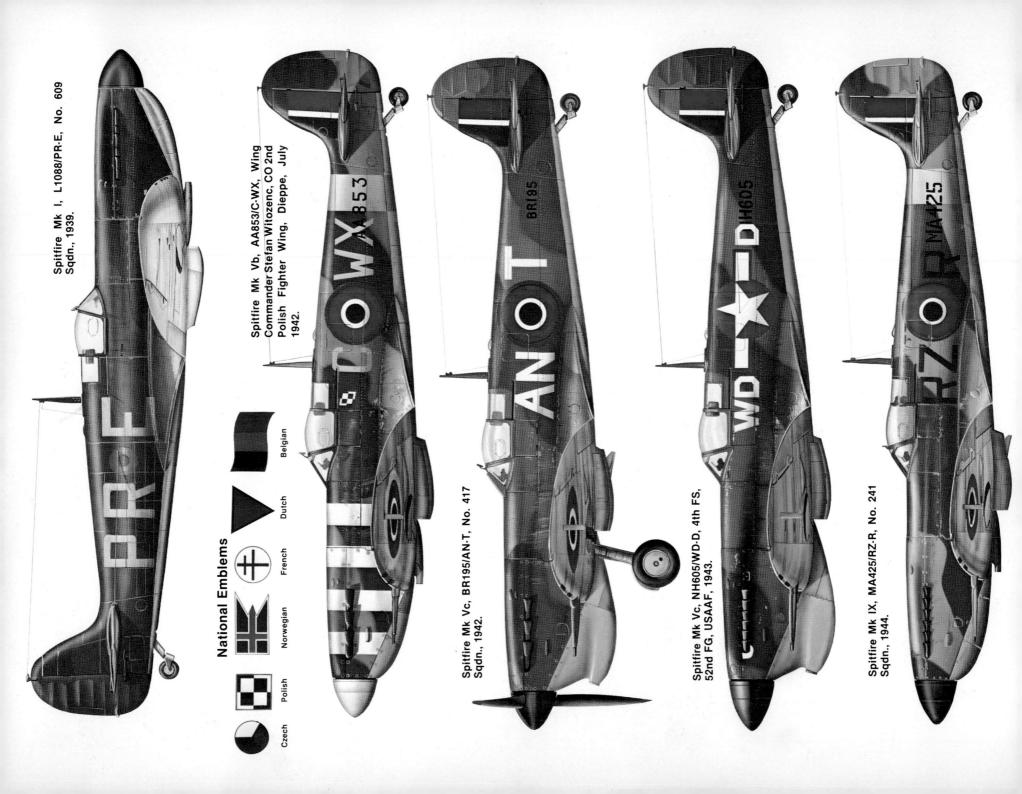

Spitfire Mk I, L1088/PR-E, No. 609 Sqdn., 1939.

Spitfire Mk Vb, AA853/C-WX, Wing Commander Stefan Witozenc, CO 2nd Polish Fighter Wing, Dieppe, July 1942.

Spitfire Mk Vc, BR195/AN-T, No. 417 Sqdn., 1942.

Spitfire Mk Vc, NH605/WD-D, 4th FS, 52nd FG, USAAF, 1943.

Spitfire Mk IX, MA425/RZ-R, No. 241 Sqdn., 1944.

National Emblems

Belgian

Dutch

French

Norwegian

Polish

Czech

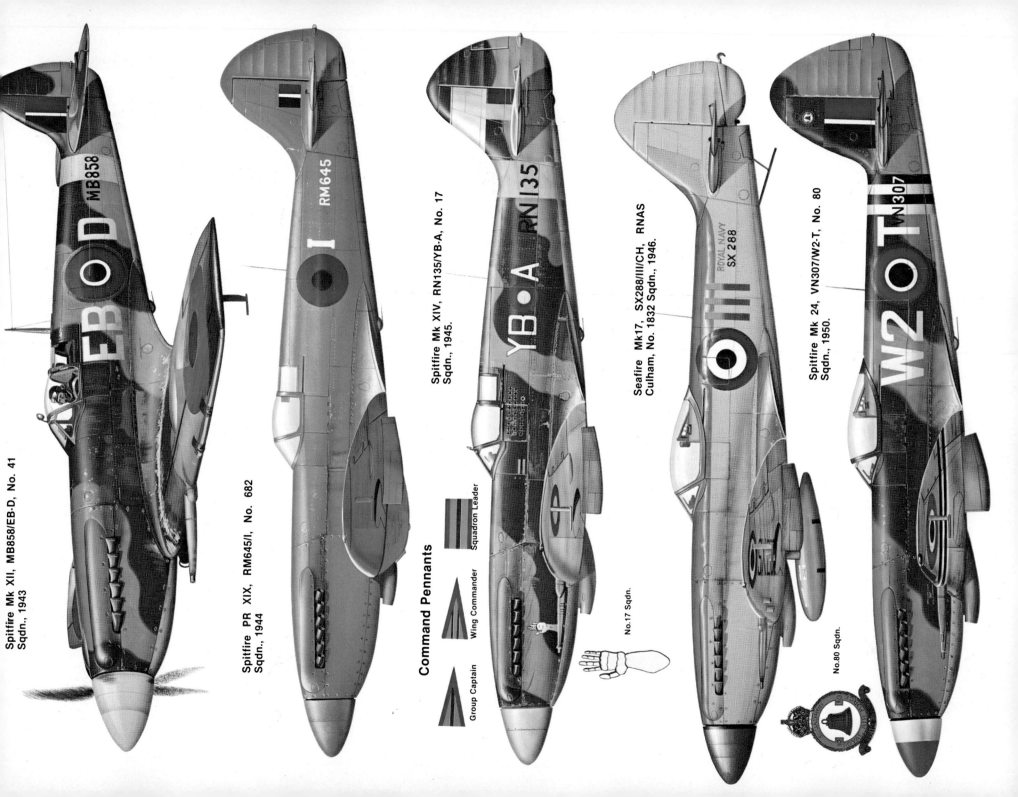

Spitfire Mk XII, MB858/EB·D, No. 41 Sqdn., 1943

Spitfire PR XIX, RM645/I, No. 682 Sqdn., 1944

Spitfire Mk XIV, RN135/YB·A, No. 17 Sqdn., 1945.

Seafire Mk17, SX288/III/CH, RNAS Culham, No. 1832 Sqdn., 1946.

Spitfire Mk 24, VN307/W2·T, No. 80 Sqdn., 1950.

Command Pennants

Squadron Leader

Wing Commander

Group Captain

No.17 Sqdn.

No.80 Sqdn.

Spitfire Mk IXc

Specifications

Dimensions: Span 36 ft. 10 in. lenght 31 ft. 0½ in. (early models), 31 ft. 4½ in. (late models); height 12 ft. 7¾ in.

Weights: Empty 5,610 lb., normal load 7,500 lb., overload 9,500 lb.

Performance: Maximum speed 408 m.p.h. at 25,000 ft., 312 m.p.h. sea level, normal cruising speed 324 m.p.h. at 20,000 ft. Initial rate of climb 4,100 ft. per min. Time to 20,000 ft. 5-7 min. Service ceiling 43,000 ft. Stalling speed (normal load) 86 m.p.h. (flaps and undercarriage up). 76 m.p.h. (flaps and undercarriage down).

Armament: 'c' or 'e' Wing, carriers could be fitted for up to 1,000 lb. in bomb load.

Mk IXc Late

Most theatres of war saw wing leaders' aircraft coded with their initials rather than the regular squadron codes, this one being the Mk IX flown by Wg. Cmdr. B. Heath in Italy. It carries a rank pennant below the windshield and is fitted with a cylindrical long range fuel tank. (Via B. Robertson)

(Above Left) Winter '44-45, and No. 317 Sqdn of the Polish AF is on standby for another ground attack sortie from a Dutch airfield, probably Grimbergen. Amid cold but clear conditions, ground crews make final preparations to a pair of Mk IXs, bombed up and ready to go. (Gen. Sikorsky Historical Institute)

Ammunition boxes stand on the wings of No.341 (Alsace) Sqdn Mk IXs, ready for action during the post-D-Day period. The Free French unit moved to France from Tangmere as part of No. 145 Wing, 2nd Tactical Air Force, in August '44, being based initially at Sommervieu. Nearest the camera is PL141. (ECPA)

'e' Wing

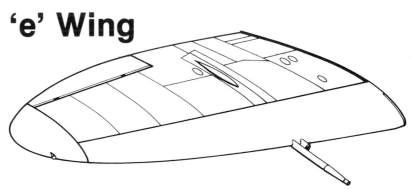

Serialled in the PT range, this Mk IX is shown on the strength of No. 340 Squadron, French Air Force, complete with 'reversed' colour roundels and rudder stripes. The 'Cross of Lorraine' marking was widely used on No. 340's wartime Spitfires, which the unit flew from December 1941 until the end of the war. (ECPA)

Mk IXe RK889 is virtually identical to the Mk VIII in appearance, the major differences being the 'e' wing with normal span ailerons and the fixed tailwheel. This plane has the integral Vokes filter in the air intake. (Vickers)

"Slipper" fuel tank

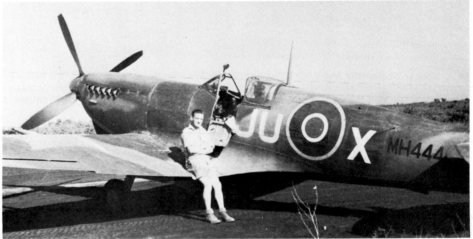

F/O A.F. Lane piloted this Mk IX MH444 of No. 111 Sqdn, seen at Lago, Italy, in March '44. (F.F. Smith)

They say that if it looks right...and in this view, Spitfire Mk IX MK126 of No. 126 Squadron certainly looks just that - every inch a thoroughbred. The place is Harrowbeer in Devon, the time, summer 1944. (Via Aeroplane)

RY·A, a Mk IX of No. 313 Sqdn. (Czech), probably at Mendlesham, Spring 1944. This is a later production IX with the broad-chord rudder. The Czech roundel is carried under the windscreen and a personal insignia on the cowl. Note also the "slipper" tank under the fuselage. (Frantisek Sazel)

(Above Right) A group of Spitfire Mk IXe fighters of the new Czech AF, seen at Budejovice soon after the end of the war. These planes now carry the Czech national colors on their vertical tails. (Dusan Mikolas)

At Kali Benteng, three white mice adorn the lower nose of this Dutch LF IX coded H-60 (ex-NH238). Flying a high level of reconnaissance, bombing, ground attack and supply missions, considering the primitive conditions in Java, No. 322 Sqdn returned home in late 1949, the last sorties taking place on 1 September. Only two Spitfires were lost during this period. (Peeters)

The three Dutch Spitfire Trainers were MK715 (H-97), BF274 (H-98) and BS147 (H-99), British serial numbers being applied below the fin flash. The trio is seen here prior to delivery. (Vickers)

Spitfire PR Mk XI

Utilizing the Merlin 61 engine, the PR XI incorporated the results of experience with early photographic reconnaissance Spitfires and was a logical development of the Mk IX fighter. Production followed the conversion of 15 Mk IXs by No. 1 Photographic Reconnaissance Unit at Benson and early examples were diverted from fighter contracts and powered by the Merlin 61, 63, or 63A. Later machines had the broad-chord rudder and in the case of the last 211 airframes, the Merlin 70 engine.

Camera provision on the PR XI was 'Universal', a fit that originated with the Types 'W',

'X' and 'Y' installations of the PR Mk IV. Obliquely-mounted cameras in blister fairings could also be attached outboard of each wheel well.

Performance of the PR XI fitted with the Merlin 70 included a maximum speed of 422 mph at 27,000 ft, with a time to 20,000 ft of five minutes.

The Spitfire PR Mk XIII was designed as a low altitude, armed fighter reconnaissance version of the PR Mk VI, and was similar to the Seafire LR IIc but with three cameras rather than the two used in the naval version. The latter also had the advantage of a four-blade rather than three-blade de Havilland propeller and enjoyed superior performance. Conversions to the PR Mk XIII were from Mks IIa, Va/b and PR VII airframes, 26 examples being completed with armament of four .303 Browning MGs. A maximum range of 700 miles could be attained with extra fuel tanks. One dozen Mk XIIIs were used by shore-based RN units and in addition, four RAF squadrons operated this version.

This PR Mk XI, developed from the Mk IX fighter, differs only slightly from the latter. Besides the unarmored windshield and lack of wing armament, note deep lower cowling. This housed a larger oil tank to allow for greater oil consumption during long photo-reconnaissance flights. (Vickers)

PR Mk XI Canopy

Spitfire PR Mk XI PL841/U of No. 681 Sqdn taxies out for take off from Alipore, Calcutta, in the hands of W/O Bill Wells, 28 December 1944. (F. F. Smith)

35

Spitfire Mk XVI

Although externally similar to the late production Mk IX, the Mk XVI was given a new mark number to distinguish its powerplant - the Merlin 266 built by the US Packard Motor Co. A low-rated Merlin 66, the engine began to reach the UK in quantity in 1944 and was installed in production Mk IXs from September.

Among the changes incorporated on the Packard Merlin (which was built to metric measurements) was an electro-hydraulically operated supercharger gear (compared to electro-pneumatic for British engines). The intercooler header tank was integral with the power unit rather than bulkhead mounted, and the oil piping run was modified.

Early machines had 'c' wing armament, later 'e', and a cut down rear fuselage with bubble canopy was standard from February 1945. Most Mk XVIs also had clipped wings for the low level role. The production total was 1,053.

Although performance was similar to that of the Mk IX, fuel tankage of the Mk XVI differed in some respects: the lower front fuselage tank held 47 gals. compared to 37 gals. for the Mk IX, and the rear fuselage tank capacity was 76 gals. with the original deep fuselage or 66 gals. with the cut down design.

'Addis Ababa', seen during factory testing, represents a standard later Spitfire Mk XVIe. Normally used at low altitudes, many XVIs had clipped wings. Late Mk XVIs and Mk IXs had the bubble canopy seen here. (Vickers)

LF Mk XVI TE274/GE-K of 349 Squadron, 1st Wing de Chasse, Belgian Air Force, after the war. The base is believed to be Beauvechain. (Via Robertson)

Clipped 'e' Wing

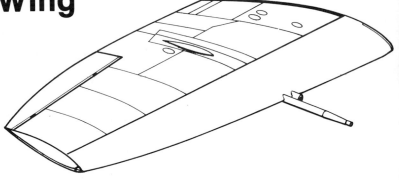

They also served...TE471, an LF Mk XVI was carrying the markings of No. 61 Operational Training Unit when it was photographed on display with a Halifax at an unknown location after the war. Storm weights attached to the Spitfire's tailwheel and wings suggest an airfield prone to high winds, probably one of the bomber bases in Lincolnshire or Yorkshire.

Production LF XVI SL576, showing the various recognition points of this mark, including the broad chord rudder, bubble canopy, clipped wings (shown here with bomb racks), whip aerial and non-retracting (castoring) tailwheel. Also, the subtle but definite bulge to the top of the engine cowling is well shown. (Vickers)

Currently preserved, TE330 is one of the relatively few Spitfire Mk XVIs remaining. Fitted with the normal span wingtips, this plane shows well the revised fuselage and later rudder, which enhanced the slender appearance of the Spitfire's fuselage. (Flight)

Spitfire Mk XII

The first variant to be powered by the Griffon engine, the Spitfire Mk XII was still basically a Mk V airframe, although it was significantly different both internally and externally. Installation of the 1735 hp Griffon IIB had been made in the Mk V prototype DP845 and the machine had been brought up to Mk XX standard as early as 1942. Fitted with clipped wings, it met the requirement for the Mk XII, which was intended primarily to combat Luftwaffe 'hit and run' raids on British coastal targets. In the forefront of such attacks was the ubiquitous Fw 190, which was once again to influence Spitfire development.

Production Mk XIIs were modified from Mk Vc/IX and VIII contracts, the first examples of the 100 machines built having the fixed tailwheel of the Mk IX, the balance the retractable unit of the Mk VIII. All had the broad chord rudder of the Mk VIII. The supercharged Griffon III was mounted ten inches further forward in the airframe than the Merlin, to give the Mk XII an overall length of 31 ft. 10 in. A four-blade Rotol propeller with either Dural or Jablo (wood composite) blades rotated clockwise when seen head-on; the Merlin rotated counter-clockwise. This meant that considerable left rudder and full left trim were required to counter the starboard swing on take-off, the Mk XII exhibiting markedly changed flying characteristics compared with Merlin-engined versions.

Wing armament was of the 'c' type intended for the Mk V as a 'universal' fit, but with the cannon mounted in the inboard positions, the outers remaining empty. Four 0.303 in Brownings completed the Mk XII's fixed armament.

Used only in the UK, the Mk XII was issued to Nos. 41 and 91 Sqdns for home defense duties beginning in January 1943. Among the modifications introduced during the Mk XII's service life was the replacement of the IFF tailplane-to-fuselage aerial by a rod aerial under the starboard wing, substitution of four, rather than five, wheel spokes, enlargement of the elevator horn balances and elimination of the upper wing bulges. The latter change was made possible by introducing bulged undercarriage doors, the wheels resting lower in their wells when retracted. Link type oleo legs were also introduced.

No. 41 Sqdn flying their Spitfire Mk XIIs. As it was an interim type pending deliveries of the more developed Mk XIV, only two squadrons flew the Mk XII. Note the shorter cowlings of these aircraft - the Mk XIV had the Griffon engine mounted farther forward. (ECPA)

Salient features of the first Griffon-engined Spitfire can be seen well in this view of MB882, one of the Mk XIIs based on the Mk VIII airframe and featuring a retractable tailwheel. It bears the markings of No. 41 Squadron, the first to receive the type in February 1943. No. 91 Sqdn followed suit in April, these two squadrons being the only units to operate the Mk XII. (IWM)

Spitfire Mk XIV

First of the Griffon-engined Spitfires to enter large scale production, the Mk XIV was still something of an interim type. Suitable for relatively quickly production, it was intended for combat at all altitudes and incorporated all the refinements of the later Merlin and early Griffon-engined machines. It was based on the Mk VIII airframe, the powerplant being the Griffon 65 or 66 with a five blade Rotol propeller. Production machines were built to F or FR standard.

All examples of the Mk XIV had a broad chord fin which was taller than that of the Mk XII (the rudder height also being increased) and fishtail exhaust stubs were eliminated in favor of the round-section type. Early production aircraft had 'c' wings; the rest had 'e' ('Universal') wings.

Use of an intercooler necessitated two underwing radiators, these being larger than the starboard wing unit of the Mk XII. Fuel capacity was boosted by 26 gals., a 13 gal. tank being fitted into each wing leading edge.

Identifiable by its cut-down rear fuselage and bubble canopy, the FR Mk XIV had a single F.24 oblique camera in the fuselage and could accommodate a 31 gal. fuel tank aft of the cockpit. Clipped wings with 'Universal' armament were usually fitted, and later production machines had an extra 7.25 in. increase in rudder chord to compensate for the loss of directional stability with the 'bubble' canopy fitted. The height of the fin was also increased and 'anti-balance' trim tabs were fitted.

F Mk XIVe variants could carry up to 1000 lbs. of bombs on fuselage and wing racks, the F Mk XIVc having its load restricted to 500 lbs. only on the fuselage rack. A total of 957 Mk XIVs was built, the first examples entering service in Europe with No. 610 (County of Chester) Sqdn, in January 1944. Subsequently 37 RAF squadrons flew it, some well into the post-war era, making the Mk XIV the most widely used of all Griffon-engined Spitfires and the only one to be used in quantity during WWII.

On 6 January 1944, No. 610 (County of Chester) Squadron took delivery of the first Mk XIVs in service. Subsequent formation flights were well covered by the cameras, resulting in pictures like this, well doing justice to one of the best-looking Spitfires of them all. From the foreground, the machines are: RB159, RB167, RB150 and RB156, the last aircraft later seeing service as SG68 in the Belgian Air Force. (IWM)

A superb study of the first production F Mk XIVc, RB140, on a factory test flight. The first version built to full Mk XIV standard, with broad chord rudder and 'c' wing armament, late examples were subsequently built with the cut down rear fuselage and bubble canopy. (Vickers)

Spitfire Mk XIVc

Specifications

Dimensions: Span, 36 ft. 10 in. Lenght 32 ft. 8 in. height 12 ft. 8 in. Wing area at standard span 244 sq. ft.

Weights: Loaded 8,375 lb. fighter version; 9,000 lb. fighter reconnaissance version with rear tank overload (F.R. version with rear tank and 90 gall. drop tank) 9,772 lb. Maximum permissible for take-off and straight-flight only 10,280 lb. (maximum permissible for landing was 8750 lb).

Performance: Maximum speed ('S' gear) 439 m.p.h. at 24,500 ft. ('M'gear) 404 m.p.h. at 11,000 ft. 357 m.p.h. at sea level. Normal cruising speed 362 m.p.h. at 20,000 ft. Rate of climb initially 4,580 ft. per min. Time to 20,000 ft. 7 min. Service ceiling 43,000 ft. Stalling speed (engine off) at 8,375 lb. 85 m.p.h. (flaps and undercarriage up), 75 m.p.h. (flaps and undercarriage down). Maximum diving speed permitted, 470 m.p.h.

Armament: 'c' or 'e' Wing (Hispano Mk.II cannon) with provision for carriage of 1 × 500 lb. AN/M58, 64 or 76 bomb or 1 × 500 lb. S.A.P. bomb or Mk. IX rocket projectiles.

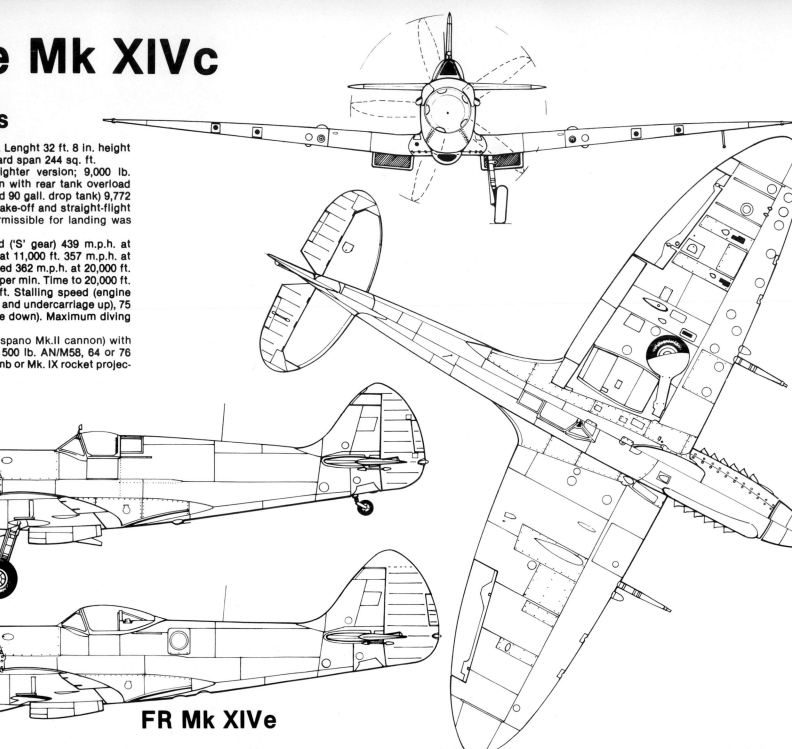

FR Mk XIVe

Storm weights hold down Mk XIV NH858 at an unrecorded Far Eastern airfield after the war. (Via H. Holmes)

(Above Right) Reachinng SEAC squadrons at the close of the war against the Japanese, Mk XIVs were in time to carry out a number of useful fighter/reconnaissance sorties before the end. One such was this FR coded 'K' and possibly serialled MV303. (RAF Museum)

Still bearing theatre identification bands on wings, tallplane and rudder, this FR Mk XIV, NH927/R has typical SEAC anonymity through lack of squadron codes. (Via Aeroplane)

FR Mk XIV

The late 1940s saw considerable use of Spitfire Mk XIVs by the Belgian Air Force, 132 examples of the type equipping both fighter squadrons and training units. This view shows three machines being used in the training role with the Ecole de Chasse with Belgian serials SG108 (ex-NH789), SG112 and SG117/IQ-M. (Via Robertson)

Spitfire Mk XVIII

Almost identical to the later Mk XIV, the Mk XVIII was the last Griffon-engined development of the original Spitfire airframe. With strengthened 'e' wing fitted with full span tips, the mark appeared in both F and FR form. Powerplant was the Griffon 65 or 67 in late production machines, the latter engine producing 2375 hp; all examples had the five blade Rotol propeller.

FR XVIIIs had provision for three cameras, one oblique and two vertical - which was the installation used in the PR XIX. Installation of the cameras required the removal of one rear fuselage fuel tank. All Mk XVIIIs had the cut-down rear fuselage and bubble canopy.

In addition to gun armament - which in the case of machine guns was of 0.5 in. caliber rather than 0.303 in. - the Mk XVIII was stressed to carry up to 1000 lbs. of bombs on fuselage and wing racks, or up to four Mk 8 or 9 rocket projectiles on underwing hardpoints.

Production of the variant ran to 300 of both F and FR types, the majority being used in the Middle and Far Eastern theatres post-war, as far as RAF service was concerned.

FR Mk XVIII TP448/GZ-? of No. 32 Squadron flying from Cyprus in 1949. Use of a question mark in place of an individual aircraft code letter was not an uncommon RAF practice during and after WWII. (Via Robertson)

Three RAF Spitfire squadrons were part of the long anti-terrorist campaign in Malaya known as 'Operation Firedog'. With No. 81 Sqdn, the FEAF reconnaissance unit, Nos. 28 and 60 Sqdns flew Mk XVIIIs on offensive sorties until January 1949 and January 1951 respectively. This photograph shows Mk XVIIIs being readied for a typical rocket strike at Kuala Lumpur on 15 July 1948, although the parent unit is not positively identified. (Via Aeroplane)

Spitfire PR Mk XIX

The need for a pressurised PR Spitfire to operate at altitudes above 38,000 ft. was filled by the PR Mk XIX, the last photo reconnaissance variant and the only one powered by a Griffon engine. Able to reach 42,000 ft. where it had a better chance of evading the German jets then challenging RAF PR flights, the Mk XIX entered service in June 1944. It was basically a Mk XIV airframe fitted with a pressure cabin, 'bowser' wing and Griffon 66 engine driving a five blade Rotol propeller. Three cameras could be fitted, one oblique and two vertical, although all three were not normally carried at once.

The first 25 aircraft lacked pressure cabins and were powered by the Griffon 65; none were initially tropicalized, although 16 were dispatched overseas, the PR XIX being intend-ed from the outset for use abroad as well as in Europe. The fuel capacity of these early machines was also different from that of aircraft powered by the Griffon 66, with only one tank fitted into each wing rather than two.

All but the last few of the subsequent 200 PR XIXs built had pressure cabins, visually distinguishable by the absence of the port side cockpit access door and the addition of a small 'pencil' air intake for the cabin compressor on the port side of the nose below the exhaust stacks.

The camera installation was two fanned vertical F.52s with 20 or 36 in. lenses; two vertical F.8 models with 20 in. lenses or two vertical F.24s with 14 in. lenses and one port-facing oblique F.24 with an 8 or 14 in. lens. Two main fuselage tanks with total fuel of 82.5 gals., plus wing tanks of 105 or 106.5 gals. gave a total capacity of 254 or 257 gals., plus auxiliary drop tanks of 30, 45, 90 or 170 gal. size. This gave production PR Mk XIXs a range of 1,085 miles on internal fuel alone at normal cruising speed, and a maximum of 1,550 miles with the 170 gal. overload tank.

A production PR Mk XIX, PM655, on a test flight. This version made the last RAF opertional Spitfire sortie in 1954 and one example is retained by the Battle of Britain Memorial Flight. (Vickers)

Flanked by Hornets, a Harvard and a Beaufighter, this view of Kai Tak, Hong Kong includes a pair of No. 81 Sqdn PR Mk XIXs on detachment there, 1952-53. (Flight)

Turkey, India and Sweden bought PR Mk XIXs after the war, one of the latter country's 50 examples being seen here, probably at South Marston. The small rear fuselage serial number 31001 indicates the first aircraft delivered and the number '11' the operational SAF wing, F11. (Aeroplane)

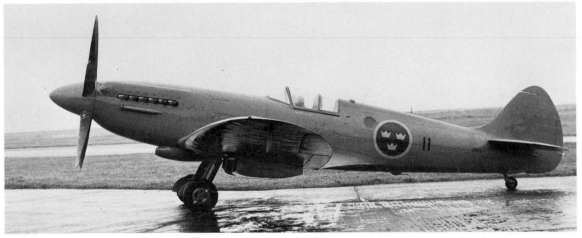

PR Mk XIX Cowling

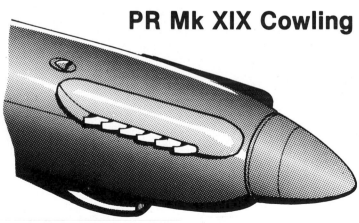

This fine shot shows one of the surviving airworthy Spitfires, PR Mk XIX PS853, painted in a camouflage finish that it never bore in RAF operational service. The photograph was taken in 1973, the aircraft having since been given an authentic 'PRU blue' color scheme. (Ministry of Defence)

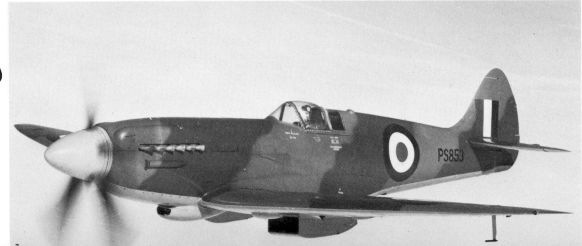

Spitfire Mk 21

Mk 21/24 Wing

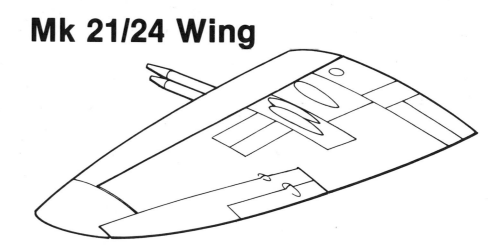

As the development of the Spitfire progressed into the later war years, features that had distinguished the series were gradually changed and with the F Mk 21, the elliptical wing gave way to a new design without the same subtle trailing edge curvature. So different was this variant in fact, that the name 'Victor' was put forward, the feeling being that the machine was no longer a Spitfire. It was in effect, the 'Super Spitfire' that had first taken tangible form in DP845, the Mk IV/XX development aircraft.

British standardization on cannon rather than machine guns for fighter armament was reflected in the Mk 21, there being no provision for machine guns. Four cannon contributed to a high airframe weight which, during series development, had crept up from 4810 lbs. empty for the Mk Ia to 7160 lbs. for the Mk 21.

To accommodate the heavier airframe, the Mk 21's undercarriage was lengthened and positioned further outboard than previously and when retracted, the mainwheels were completely enclosed by doors for the first time. Production deliveries commenced in September 1944, Castle Bromwich building some 100 examples - a small fraction of at least 3,000 originally ordered.

The powerplant for the Mk 21 was the Griffon 61 or 85 of 2045 hp with a five-blade Rotol, or two three blade contra-rotating Rotol propellers respectively. The blade diameter was increased to 11 ft. as a result of better ground clearance offered by the longer undercarriage.

An excellent flying view of LA328, an F.21 of No. 600 (County of London) Squadron, Royal Auxiliary Air Force, during the halcyon days of the late 1940s when flying machines like this on weekends made a man's weekly task lighter. (Flight)

A pair of F.21s of No. 615 (County of Surrey) Squadron scramble from Biggin Hill, where the squadron was reformed in July 1946. At left, RAV-B is LA313, with LA191 coded 'D'. (Aeroplane)

Seen on the ground, Mk 21 LA188 might be mistaken for a Mk XIV. The major difference is the new wing with the blunt tip, four cannon, much larger underwing radiators and outer wheel well doors. (Vickers)

Spitfire Mk 22/24

Penultimate development of the Spitfire under that name, the Mk 22 initially differed little from the Mk 21 apart from having a cut down rear fuselage and bubble canopy, but later machines incorporated Spiteful-type vertical tails and larger tailplanes. The powerplant could be either the Griffon 61 with a five-blade Rotol propeller or the Griffon 85 with a six-blade contraprop installation, other specifications being identical to that of the Mk 21 except for the maximum permissable weight, which rose to 11,350 lb. for the Mk 22 (11,290 lb. for the Mk 21).

Production began on 21 March 1945 and 260 were built. Most were used by Auxiliary Air Force squadrons although others saw service overseas in the hands of foreign air forces.

Whereas the Mk 22 was stressed to carry up to 1,500 lbs. of bombs, the Mk 24 could also carry rocket projectiles but was otherwise similar. Detail changes included an electrical rather than pneumatic gun-firing system and other modifications to equipment. With the war over the urgency to reequip the front line squadrons was gone and it took some two years to complete the final Spitfire order for 54 Mk 24s. Only No. 80 Squadron used the type in any numbers, first as part of the occupation force in Germany and subsequently in the Far East, where some machines were marked with black and white stripes in the event of their use on the fringes of the Korean war.

Ordered as one of the prototype Spitfire F.21s, SX549 was apparently not used as such. The revised wing shape of the late production Spitfires is evident in this view, which also shows the serial number chalked, rather than painted, on the rear fuselage. (Vickers)

This shot of a new Mk22 shows the wheel well doors and four cannon armament. The bubble canopy was the same as that adopted for the Mk XVI and late Mk XIVs and XVIIIs. (Vickers)

Spitfire F Mk 22/24

Specifications

Dimensions: Span 36 ft. 11 in., length 32 ft. 8 in., wing area 234.6 sq. ft.

Weights: Empty 7,160 lb., normal loaded 9,900 lb. maximum permissible (with 170 gall. drop tank) 11,290 lb.

Performance: Maximum speed at 19,00 ft. 450 m.p.h., at 25,000 ft. 449 m.p.h., sea level 390 m.p.h. Maximum rate of climb 4,900 ft. per min. Service ceiling 43,000 ft. Range (normal) 580 miles at 230 m.p.h. at 20,000 ft. (70 gall. drop tank) 965 miles. Maximum diving speed 520 m.p.h.

Armament: 4 × 20 mm. British Hispano Mk. II cannon with 175 r.p.g. inboard and 150 r.p.g. outboard.

Mk 21

Above and below: These two photographs illustrate the difference between early and late production F.22s, both machines being from the first production batch in the serial range PK312-356. Built with F.21 vertical tail surfaces, PK312 was subsequently fitted with the larger Spiteful-type tail, as shown here in March 1945. (Vickers)

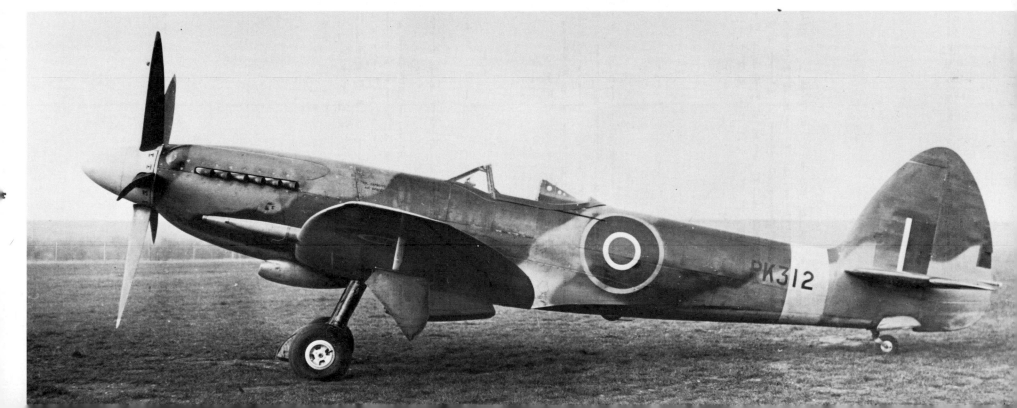

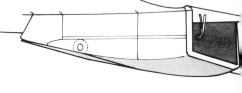

Part of the third F.22 production batch, PK431 is shown at Castle Bromwich in a state to delight the model-maker! Note the shape of the new wing and the non-standard four cannon installation. (Vickers)

Mk 21-24
deep radiator

Coffman cartridge starters make their characteristic smoke as No. 1 Squadron, Southern Rhodesia Air Force prepares to fly its Spitfire F.22s from Salisbury Airport. As can be seen by the tail of the aircraft on the left, serial numbers given to the 22 aircraft delivered were SR58-68 and SR79-89. (Via Robertson)

The last RAF squadron to fly the Spitfire in the operational fighter role was No. 80, which also claimed the distinction of the only unit to be fully equipped with the Mk 24. Transferring from Germany in 1949, it flew armed patrols from Hong Kong until early 1952. This photo shows the squadron's aircraft at Kai Tak, probably soon after arrival.(Via Robertson)

Seafire Mk Ib

Transfer of an initial batch of 48 RAF Spitfire Mk Vb aircraft to the Royal Navy commenced late in 1941 and was followed by a further 118 machines. Enabling the Navy to gain valuable experience in operating the type from carriers, 45 of the first batch had 'A' frame arrester hooks and internal detail changes to fit them for this purpose. As such they were known as 'hooked Spitfires'. These limited modifications had little adverse effect on performance compared to the standard Spitfire Mk Vb, empty weight being only some 5 per cent higher. Used mostly for training, these early aircraft were joined by the first Seafire to be known as such, the Seafire Mk Ib.

As an interim Naval version, the Seafire Ib's modifications - also from Mk V airframes -were still limited. An arrester hook was fitted, together with slinging points and local strengthening to permit handling aboard carriers and aircraft lighters, naval high frequency r/t and naval IFF radio equipment and a receiver for a Type 72 homing beacon. No provision was made for wing-folding. Conversion work was undertaken by two Supermarine subcontractors in Hampshire, Air Service Training at Hamble and Cunliffe-Owen at Eastleigh, 116 aircraft being modified to Seafire Ib standard.

The sole front-line Royal Navy unit to be fully equipped with the Seafire Ib was 801 Squadron aboard HMS Furious from October 1942 until September 1944. Concurrent production of the Seafire Mk IIc enabled the bulk of Seafire Ib examples to be used for training, although 842 Sqdn received a number to augment strength in the summer of 1943 at the time of the Salerno operations.

Seafire 'A' Frame Arrester Hook

Under expert guidance from the 'batsman' on the right hand side of the deck and the critical eye of deck handling parties, a Seafire approaches the moment of truth aboard HMS Formidable in January 1943. The Seafires are from 885 Squadron, those positioned on the deck-edge outriggers including MB345/K and MB360/G, with fully coded Ø6-B in between. Both aircraft with visible serials are Mk Ibs. (IWM)

Seafire Mk IIc

As the first true production version of the Seafire, the Mk IIc was offset from Spitfire V contracts and 262 examples were built by both Supermarine and Westland. The main difference from the early Seafires was the addition of catapult spools. Powerplant for the F IIc was as for the Ib: a Merlin 45 or 46 of 1470 and 1415 hp respectively, all aircraft having provision for 'c' wing armament.

As noted, production was parallel with that of the Mk Ib, the first examples being taken on charge by the Navy on the same day, 15 June 1942. However, as the increased weight of the Mk V Spitfire went up even further in the Seafire II equivalent, the Vokes filter fairing was rarely used, even in the Mediterranean. Poor level speed and rate of climb were offset to some extent by dispensing with the fairing, the Navy accepting increased engine wear as a result. An engine boost modification was also introduced, to give +16 lb. sq. in. manifold pressure at low level, although as the same change had been incorporated on the Mk Ib, the IIc was still the slower of the two.

Experiments with the Seafire IIc included the fitting of RATOG (Rocket Assisted Take Off Gear), although it was not used operationally, and attachment points for 5 in. rockets, which were. A 500 lb. bomb could be carried on the fuselage centerline rack.

Seafire L IIc

To boost the Seafire's low altitude performance, it was decided in late 1942 to install a new engine, the 1645 hp Merlin 32. Following successful trials in December, the new engine was substituted on Mk IIc aircraft from March 1943. Offering more engine power from a smaller, cropped supercharger impeller, the Merlin 32 had boost increased to + 18 lb. sq. in. to give 1640 hp at full throttle. A four blade Rotol propeller was fitted. These and other changes gave the L IIc an outstanding low-level performance that was far in excess of any other naval fighter of the war, maximum speed at 5,000 ft. being 333 mph.

An 808 Sqdn Seafire L IIc LR691 drifting off the flight deck of a carrier, believed to be HMS Hunter, in February 1944. Then part of No. 3 Naval Fighter Wing, 808's flying was of a training, rather than operational, nature until June 1944. (L. Beckford)

Seafire LR IIc

With an RAF equivalent in the PR Mk XIII, the Seafire LR IIc was an L IIc equipped with one oblique F.24 camera mounted in the fuselage. Powerplant was the Merlin 32 with a four-blade propeller. Some 30 conversions are believed to have been made, the type entering service late in 1943.

Along with 808 Sqdn, 807 Sqdn's Seafire L IIs were also training in early 1944, but as part of No. 4 NFW. Taken from the aft port side of one of the three carriers embarking the wing in April 1944 - Hunter, Attacker and Stalker - this Seafire prepares to land. (L. Beckford)

Seafire Development

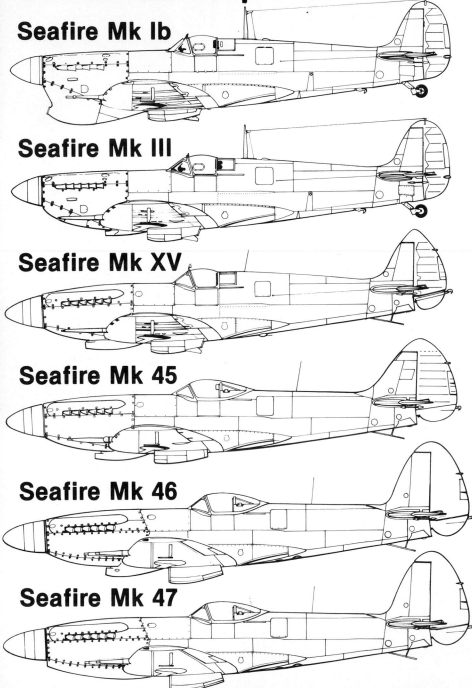

Seafire Mk Ib

Seafire Mk III

Seafire Mk XV

Seafire Mk 45

Seafire Mk 46

Seafire Mk 47

Seafire Mk III

The obvious need for wing-folding on RN Seafires was realized on the Mk III, a medium to high level fighter which could be deployed on the smaller British carriers in greater numbers than was possible with fixed-wing aircraft. Although non-folding wings had not proved to be a great problem, ships with deck elevators too small to take a full-span Seafire had had to resort to deck 'hangarage' with obvious disadvantages.

Experimentally test flown as early as the winter of 1939-40, the folding wing system incorporated on the Mk III was a simple double break of the wing on each side. The main upward fold break was just inside the inner cannon bay and the tip folded downward at the point where it joined the wing proper. Actual folding was carried out manually, the wing being secured by telescopic jury struts.

Fitted with the Merlin 55, 55M, or 32 in F, L and FR form respectively, the Seafire III proved to be an excellent aircraft well able to meet naval requirements at medium to high altitudes. Weight saving was made by deletion of the outboard cannon bay on the 'c' wing and a number of machines also had the Martin-Baker Patent Belt-Feed Mechanism, which was more compact than the original drum-feed magazine and required only slim tear drop fairings in place of the large blisters previously necessary.

The Seafire III was produced by Westland and Cunliffe-Owen, the former concern's first 30 and the latter's first two having fixed 'c' wings and being redesignated Mk IIc (Hybrid), although folding wings were subsequently fitted.

Seafire L Mk IIIc

As noted above, the L III variant had the Merlin 55M engine, with multi-ejector exhaust stacks and cropped supercharger impeller which provided 1585 hp at 2750 ft. The Vokes Aero-Vee air filter over the carburetor intake was fitted from the 90th example built. Armament modifications to later Mk IIIs included the lighter Mk V Hispano cannon and 'zero-length' rocket launchers, and all Mk III variants were cleared to carry a 500 lb. bomb on the centerline rack.

The final variant of the Seafire III series was the FR III, 129 of which were completed by Cunliffe-Owen with two F.24 fuselage cameras. Some aircraft were also modified to FR III standard by Westland. The grand total of Seafire IIIs built, in all versions, was 1218, plus 32 Mk IIc (Hybrid), this type being the final Merlin-engined Seafire to see service.

October 1944 was a period of action for 807 Squadron, operating from HMS Hunter in the Aegean. A number of anti-shipping sorties by Seafires were very successful, 807 in company with 809 Sqdn sinking two 1,000 ton freighters and damaging other vessels. Here, a Seafire L III takes off, armed with a 500 lb. bomb on the fuselage rack. (L. Beckford)

Nose-over for Seafire L III PR171/D5-J of 807 Sqdn aboard HMS Hunter in the Malacca Strait, May 1945. Both machines visible here have reduced size roundels without red centers and white identification bands, in accordance with South East Asia Command instructions. (L. Beckford)

Based at Katukurunda, Ceylon, March 1945, Seafires of 807 and 809 Sqdns RN disembarked from their carriers to fly with Far East Air Force Spitfire squadrons to gain operational experience with strike and tactical reconnaissance sorties over jungle terrain. This view shows a 250 lb. bomb being attached to the centerline rack of a Seafire FR III. (L. Beckford)

Seafire F XV

The sole wartime version of the Seafire series to be powered by the Griffon engine, the Seafire F XV was a marriage of four Spitfire marks with the wings of the Seafire L III. The fuselage was basically that of the Spitfire Vb with the enlarged fin and rudder and retractable tailwheel of the Mk VIII with the Mk IX's wing root fuel tanks, and the Griffon engine installation and accessories of the Mk XII, although the powerplant was tailored to naval requirements.

Designated Griffon VI, this engine gave 1815 hp with increased boost pressure for take off and offered a sustained rate of climb at low to medium altitudes. Internal fuel of 100 gals. capacity was 15 gals. more than any previous Seafire, but only 50 gals. could be carried externally due to stress limitations on the undercarriage. Recognition features of the Seafire XV included twin underwing radiators, and fairings on the upper engine cowling covering enlarged rocker boxes. Late production machines were fitted with the 'sting' arrestor hook of the Seafire III.

Problems with the opposite propeller rotation of the Griffon led to numerous difficulties in service, operational use not beginning until September 1945. So difficult was the Seafire XV to operate from carriers that it was prohibited from embarked flying in mid-1946, pending modifications to the supercharger clutch. These were carried out in January 1947.

Seafire 17

Reflecting development of the Spitfire/Seafire series in general, the Seafire 17 had a cut down rear fuselage with a bubble canopy but was externally similar to the Seafire XV. The last 30 XVs had the cut down fuselage, but for naval purposes, they were clearly inferior to the Seafire 17, which had other less obvious modifications making it a much more effective aircraft for carrier operations.

Principally, the undercarriage was strengthened and lengthened to give the oleos a longer stroke, improving ground clearance for the propeller blade tips. Built in F and FR form, the Seafire 17 carried two F.24 cameras in the fuselage, or a 33 gal. fuel tank aft of the pilot's seat. This capacity was increased by a 50 gal. centerline drop tank and wet points for two 22.5 gal. slipper tanks under each outer wing panel. These tanks were jettisonable but could be retained for all maneuvers and enabled a bomb to be carried on the centerline rack. Two 250 lb. bombs could also be attached to wing racks inboard of each slipper or 'combat' tank, making the Seafire 17 a far more useful fighter which could have been very effective during the closing stages of the war.

As it was, the Seafire 17 did not enter service until 1946, but it served in first- and second-line roles until 1954.

Seafire III Folding Wing

With the war over, HMS Implacable embarked 801 Squadron with new Seafire XVs collected in Australia in the autumn of 1945. Before the ill-fated Mk XV was banned from carrier flying, 801 and other units attempted to overcome the aircraft's unreliability. Seen here are 801's aircraft aboard Implacable, marked with the insignia style adopted for the British Pacific Fleet squadrons. (Via H. Holmes)

The work up period with the Seafire XV undertaken by 801 Squadron was hampered by incidents like this. Shedding half its landing gear and drop tank, N-132 is caught seconds before it slams back on Implacable's flight deck. (Via H. Holmes)

Seafire 45

The navalized equivalent of the Spitfire Mk 21, the Seafire 45 was still an interim type pending satisfactory installation of the two-stage supercharged Griffon 60 series engine in the Spitfire Mk VIII fuselage with a new wing design. The prototype Seafire 45 was in fact a Spitfire Mk 21 airframe, TM379, suitably modified with naval equipment, including a sting-type arrester hook. The wings were non-folding.

Not intended as front-line equipment, the Seafire 45 still exhibited the undesirable characteristics of the Seafire XV, the five blade propeller making the tendency to swing even worse and it was virtually impossible to fly in a straight line. Maintenance was also lengthy.

Nevertheless, the aircraft's potential performance was an improvement on earlier marks of Seafire, and armament was increased to four 20mm cannon. Only 50 examples were built, the type's difficult handling qualities making its service life very limited, even in second line roles.

The penultimate Seafire variant was the F/FR 45, represented here by LA429, one of 50 built at Castle Bromwich, and the only Seafires produced there. Not a success, the Mk 45 found little service use even with second line units. (Vickers)

Seafire Mk 46

With its nearest direct equivalent in the Spitfire Mk 22, the Seafire FR 46 was still very much a specialized naval fighter - as was the entire Seafire line. At last, the contra-rotating propeller arrangement solved the torque problems with the Griffon engine, improving the handling sufficiently to enable the aircraft to be embarked aboard carriers. Navalization included provision for RATOG, catapult strops in the wheel wells and wet points for two 22.5 gal. slipper tanks, the latter pushing the total fuel capacity to 228 gals.

As an interim type, the FR 46 gave way to the FR 47 after 24 had been built; none were issued to front line units.

Seafire FR 47

The ultimate Seafire model, the FR 47 incorporated all the innovations and improvements found necesary for sustained naval operations frm carriers. An excellent aircraft in most respects, it represented the peak of Griffon engine development as fitted to the Spitfire/Seafire airframe, with a resulting performance better than the early jet fighters.

A deeper under nose fairing housed the ram-air supercharger intake which was positioned aft of the spinner instead of in line with the wing leading edge and the Spiteful fin and rudder unit was standard. Wing folding was accomplished by hand on the first 14 production machines; thereafter hydraulic jacks and locks were provided. A 500 lb.bomb could be carried on wing hardpoints which could be substituted for launchers for eight 60 lb. rockets. Alternatively a Mk IX depth charge could be carried.

The powerplant for the FR 47 was usually the Griffon 88 of 2350 hp fitted with Rolls-Royce fuel injection, although a few early machines had the Griffon 87 with a carburetor-type fuel system. A 90 gal. flush fitting centerline tank boosted overload fuel capacity to 318 gals. to give a range of 1000 miles. Performance figures included a maximum speed of 451 mph at 20,000 ft. and a ceiling of 43,100 ft.

Widening of the undercarriage track by 1 ft. meant that the type was far more stable on deck than any of the other Griffon-engined Seafires, and it was a pleasant aircraft to deck land.

Spitfire/Seafire production ended with the completion of the last Seafire 47 in March 1949, 12 years and nine months after the first flight of the Type 300. During that time no fewer than 20,351 Spitfires and 2,408 Seafires were built.

Seafire F. 47 Cowling

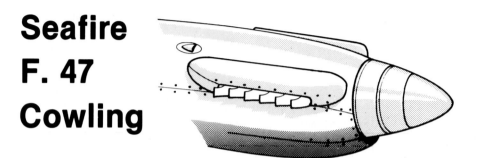

Demonstrating rocket-assisted take-off to the obvious interest of a large air show crowd, this Seafire FR 47 is VP474 of 1833 Squadron, Royal Naval Volunteer Reserve. It joined the unit at Bramcote - as indicated by the 'BR' fin code - with 11 others in the autumn of 1952. (Flight)

Seafire Mk 47

Specifications

Dimensions: Span 36 ft. 11 in., length 34 ft. 4 in., height 12 ft. 9 in. Span (wings folded) 19 ft. 1 in. Wing area (gross) 243.6 sq. ft.

Weights: Empty 7,625 lb., loaded 10,200 lb., maximum permissible 12,750 lb. Wing loading (loaded weight) 42-5 lb. per sq. ft.

Performance: Maximum speed 451 m.p.h. at 20,000 ft., maximum at 5,000 ft. 401 m.p.h. Rate of climb (initial) 4,800 ft. per min. Time to 20,000 ft. 4.8 min. Range (normal) 405 miles with allowance for take-off and 15 min. combat time; (maximum) 1,475 miles. Service ceiling 43,100 ft. Stalling speed (at loaded weight) 86-88 m.p.h. (undercarriage and flaps up), 74-76 m.p.h. (undercarriage and flaps down).

Armament: 4 × 20 mm. British Hispano Mk. V cannon. Provision for carriage of 1 × 500 lb. or 1 × 250 lb. bomb under each wing, or 8 × 60 lb. rocket projectiles or a Mk. IX depth charge.